Daily Meditation Tracker Log Book

AF422960

This logbook belongs to

Personal Data

Name : _______________________________________

Phone : _______________________________________

Address : _______________________________________

____

Incase of Emergency
Please Contact

Name : _______________________________________

Phone : _______________________________________

Address : _______________________________________

____

Essential Contacts

Doctor : _______________________________________

Pharmacy : _______________________________________

Eye Clinic : _______________________________________

Dentist : _______________________________________

Name : _______________________ Name : _______________________

Call : _______________________ Call : _______________________

Work : _______________________ Work : _______________________

Home : _______________________ Home : _______________________

Email : _______________________ Email : _______________________

Other : _______________________ Other : _______________________

Name : _______________________ Name : _______________________

Call : _______________________ Call : _______________________

Work : _______________________ Work : _______________________

Home : _______________________ Home : _______________________

Email : _______________________ Email : _______________________

Other : _______________________ Other : _______________________

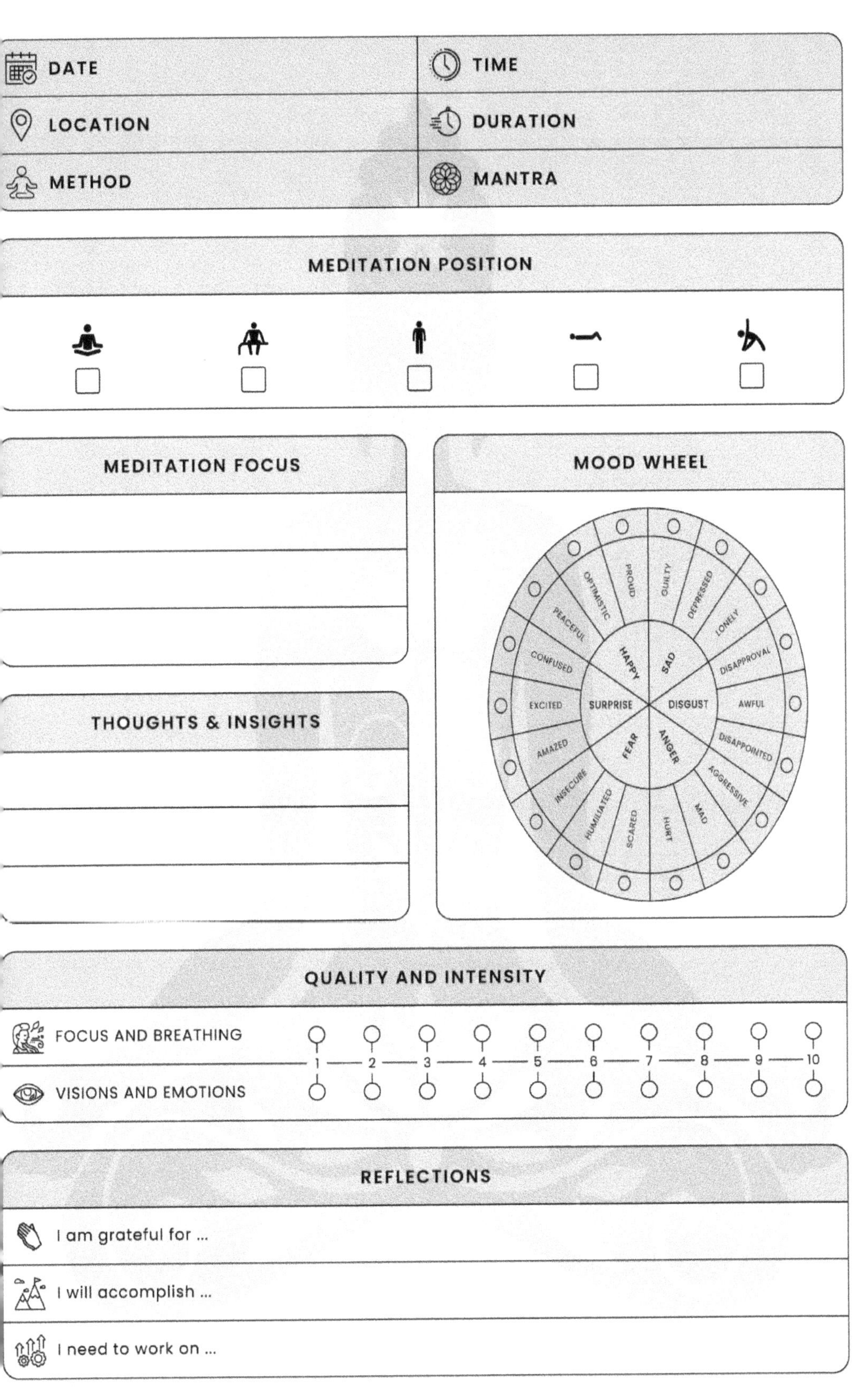

DATE
TIME
LOCATION
DURATION
METHOD
MANTRA
MEDITATION POSITION
MEDITATION FOCUS
MOOD WHEEL
OPTIMISTIC
PROUD
GUILTY
DEPRESSED
PEACEFUL
LONELY
CONFUSED
HAPPY
SAD
DISAPPROVAL
EXCITED
SURPRISE
DISGUST
AWFUL
AMAZED
FEAR
ANGER
DISAPPOINTED
INSECURE
AGGRESSIVE
HUMILIATED
SCARED
HURT
MAD
THOUGHTS & INSIGHTS
QUALITY AND INTENSITY
FOCUS AND BREATHING
1 2 3 4 5 6 7 8 9 10
VISIONS AND EMOTIONS
REFLECTIONS
I am grateful for ...
I will accomplish ...
I need to work on ...

Notes

WHAT I LIKED

____

____

____

____

WHAT I DID NOT LIKE

____

____

____

____

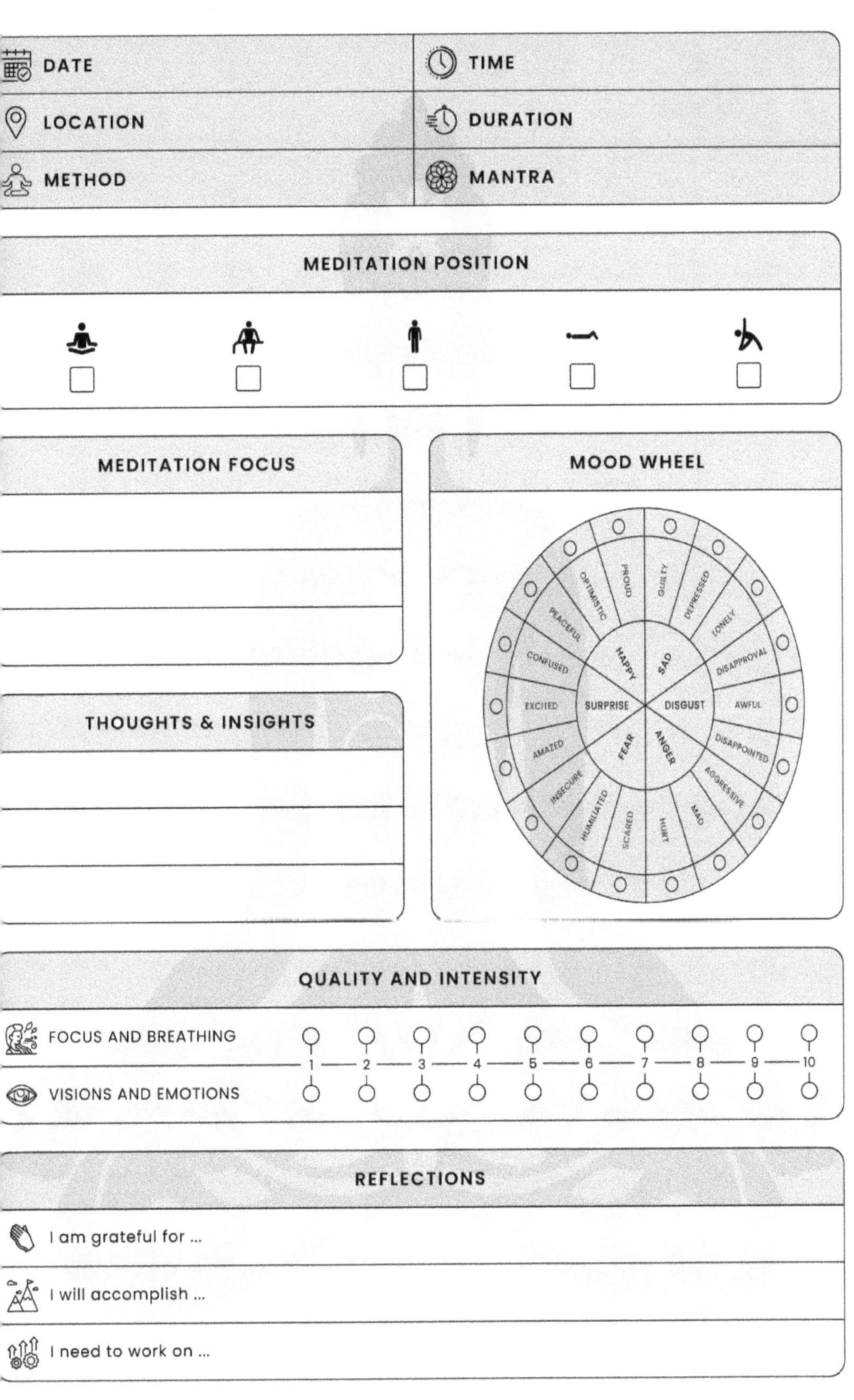

DATE	TIME
LOCATION	DURATION
METHOD	MANTRA

MEDITATION POSITION

MEDITATION FOCUS

THOUGHTS & INSIGHTS

MOOD WHEEL

QUALITY AND INTENSITY

FOCUS AND BREATHING

1 — 2 — 3 — 4 — 5 — 6 — 7 — 8 — 9 — 10

VISIONS AND EMOTIONS

REFLECTIONS

I am grateful for ...

I will accomplish ...

I need to work on ...

Notes

WHAT I LIKED

WHAT I DID NOT LIKE

DATE	TIME
LOCATION	DURATION
METHOD	MANTRA

MEDITATION POSITION

☐ ☐ ☐ ☐ ☐

MEDITATION FOCUS

MOOD WHEEL

THOUGHTS & INSIGHTS

QUALITY AND INTENSITY

FOCUS AND BREATHING

1 — 2 — 3 — 4 — 5 — 6 — 7 — 8 — 9 — 10

VISIONS AND EMOTIONS

REFLECTIONS

I am grateful for ...

I will accomplish ...

I need to work on ...

Notes

WHAT I LIKED

WHAT I DID NOT LIKE

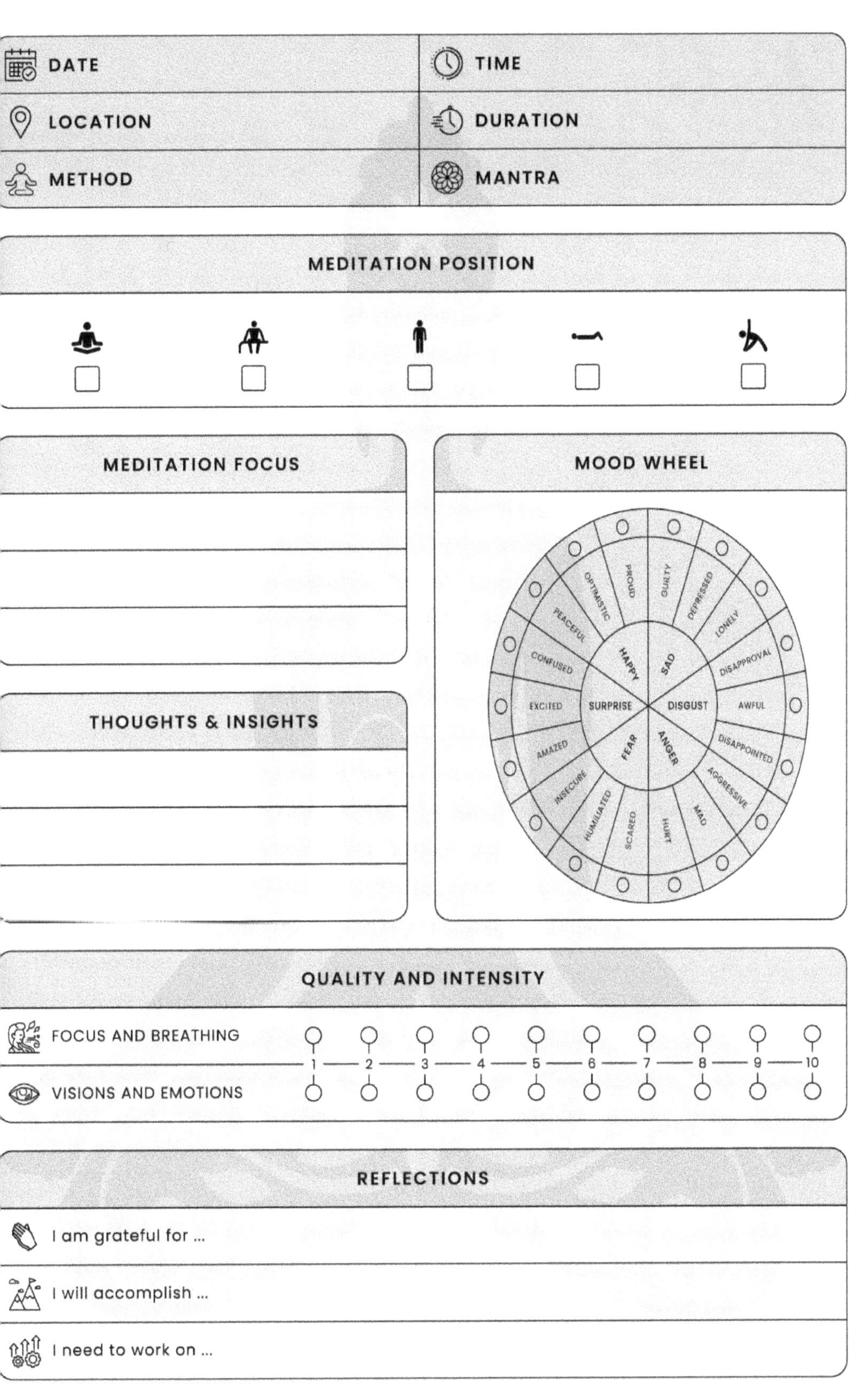

DATE
TIME
LOCATION
DURATION
METHOD
MANTRA

MEDITATION POSITION

MEDITATION FOCUS

MOOD WHEEL

OPTIMISTIC
PROUD
GUILTY
DEPRESSED
PEACEFUL
LONELY
CONFUSED
HAPPY
SAD
DISAPPROVAL
EXCITED
SURPRISE
DISGUST
AWFUL
AMAZED
FEAR
ANGER
DISAPPOINTED
INSECURE
AGGRESSIVE
HUMILIATED
SCARED
HURT
MAD

THOUGHTS & INSIGHTS

QUALITY AND INTENSITY

FOCUS AND BREATHING
1 — 2 — 3 — 4 — 5 — 6 — 7 — 8 — 9 — 10
VISIONS AND EMOTIONS

REFLECTIONS

I am grateful for ...

I will accomplish ...

I need to work on ...

Notes

WHAT I LIKED

WHAT I DID NOT LIKE

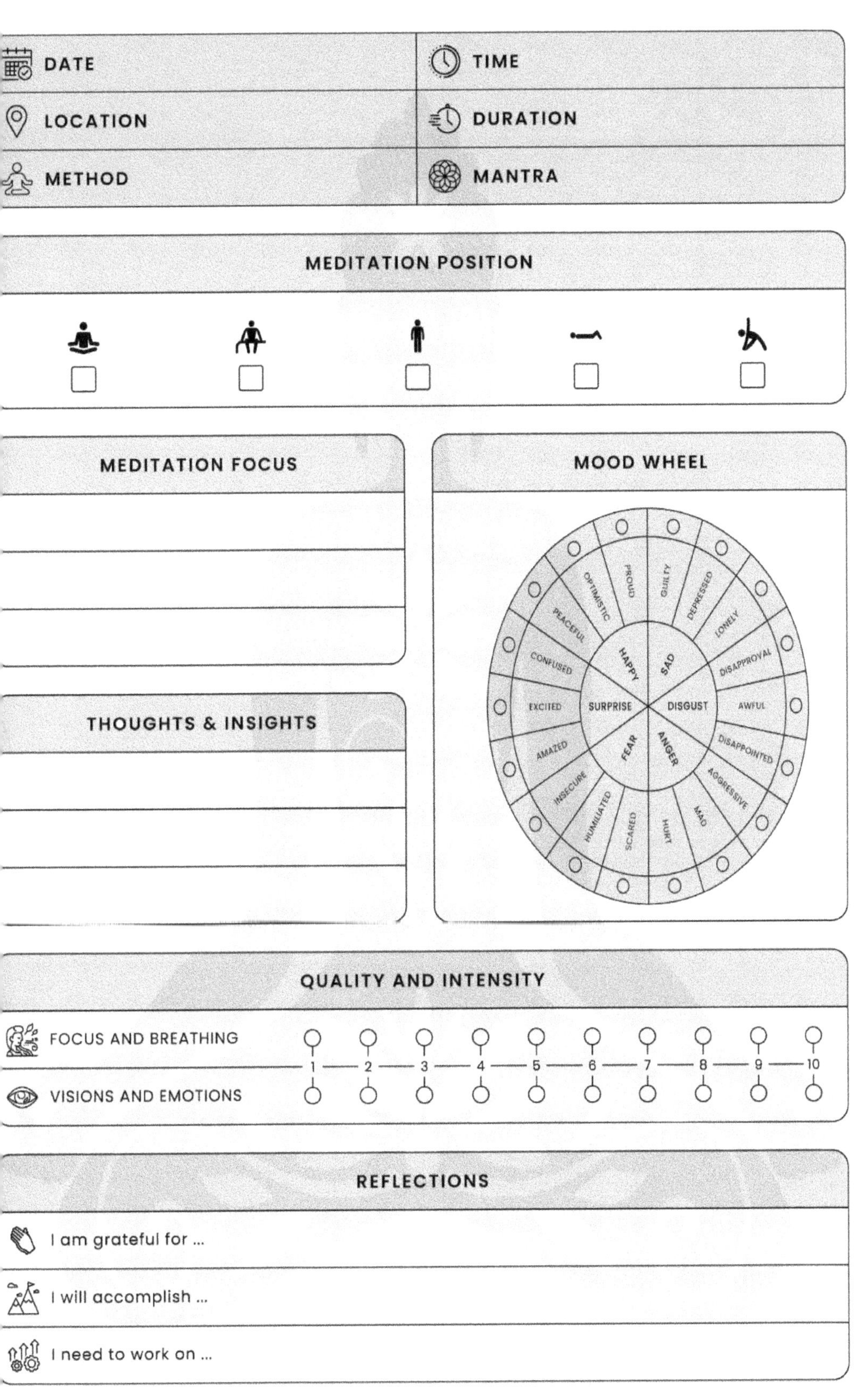

DATE
TIME
LOCATION
DURATION
METHOD
MANTRA
MEDITATION POSITION
MEDITATION FOCUS
MOOD WHEEL
OPTIMISTIC
PROUD
GUILTY
DEPRESSED
PEACEFUL
LONELY
CONFUSED
HAPPY
SAD
DISAPPROVAL
EXCITED
SURPRISE
DISGUST
AWFUL
AMAZED
FEAR
ANGER
DISAPPOINTED
INSECURE
AGGRESSIVE
HUMILIATED
SCARED
HURT
MAD
THOUGHTS & INSIGHTS
QUALITY AND INTENSITY
FOCUS AND BREATHING
1 — 2 — 3 — 4 — 5 — 6 — 7 — 8 — 9 — 10
VISIONS AND EMOTIONS
REFLECTIONS
I am grateful for ...
I will accomplish ...
I need to work on ...

Notes

WHAT I LIKED

WHAT I DID NOT LIKE

DATE	TIME
LOCATION	DURATION
METHOD	MANTRA

MEDITATION POSITION

☐ ☐ ☐ ☐ ☐

MEDITATION FOCUS

THOUGHTS & INSIGHTS

MOOD WHEEL

QUALITY AND INTENSITY

FOCUS AND BREATHING

1 — 2 — 3 — 4 — 5 — 6 — 7 — 8 — 9 — 10

VISIONS AND EMOTIONS

REFLECTIONS

I am grateful for ...

I will accomplish ...

I need to work on ...

Notes

WHAT I LIKED

WHAT I DID NOT LIKE

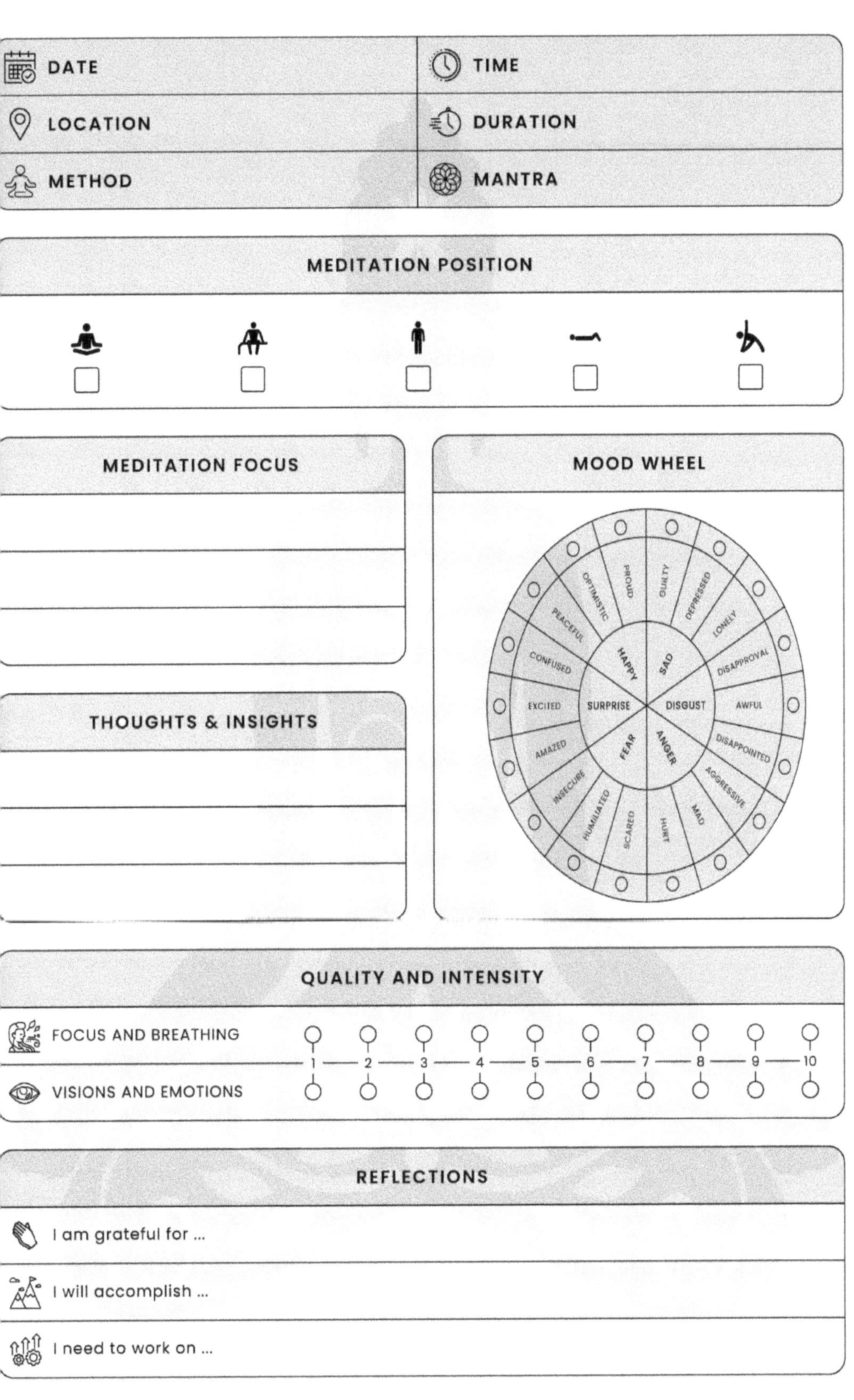

DATE
TIME
LOCATION
DURATION
METHOD
MANTRA

MEDITATION POSITION

MEDITATION FOCUS

MOOD WHEEL

OPTIMISTIC
PROUD
GUILTY
DEPRESSED
PEACEFUL
LONELY
CONFUSED
HAPPY
SAD
DISAPPROVAL
EXCITED
SURPRISE
DISGUST
AWFUL
AMAZED
FEAR
ANGER
DISAPPOINTED
INSECURE
AGGRESSIVE
HUMILIATED
SCARED
HURT
MAD

THOUGHTS & INSIGHTS

QUALITY AND INTENSITY

FOCUS AND BREATHING
1 2 3 4 5 6 7 8 9 10
VISIONS AND EMOTIONS

REFLECTIONS

I am grateful for ...

I will accomplish ...

I need to work on ...

Notes

WHAT I LIKED

WHAT I DID NOT LIKE

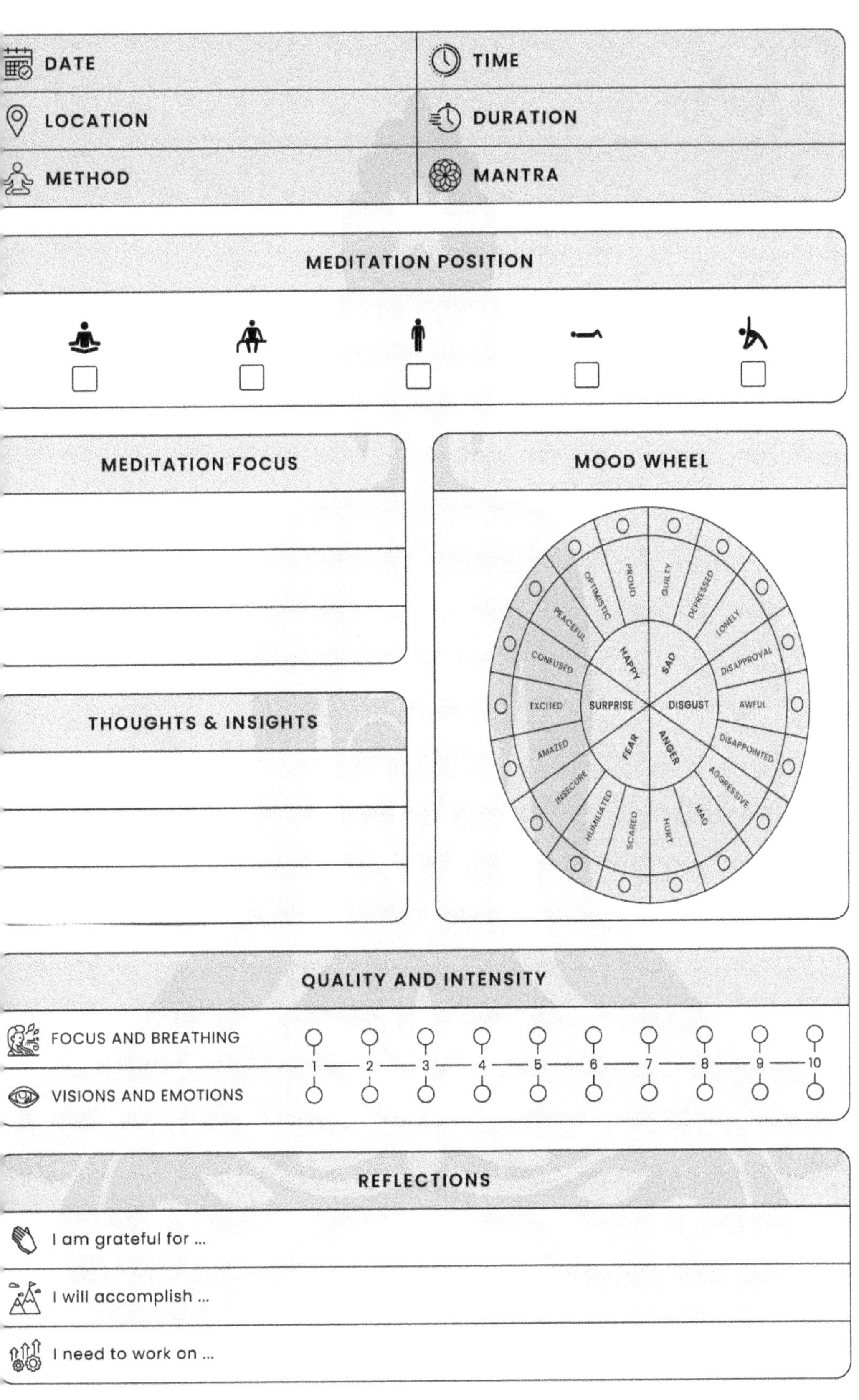
DATE
TIME
LOCATION
DURATION
METHOD
MANTRA

MEDITATION POSITION

MEDITATION FOCUS

MOOD WHEEL

OPTIMISTIC
PROUD
GUILTY
DEPRESSED
PEACEFUL
LONELY
CONFUSED
DISAPPROVAL
HAPPY
SAD
EXCITED
SURPRISE
DISGUST
AWFUL
AMAZED
FEAR
ANGER
DISAPPOINTED
INSECURE
AGGRESSIVE
HUMILIATED
SCARED
HURT
MAD

THOUGHTS & INSIGHTS

QUALITY AND INTENSITY

FOCUS AND BREATHING
1 — 2 — 3 — 4 — 5 — 6 — 7 — 8 — 9 — 10
VISIONS AND EMOTIONS

REFLECTIONS

I am grateful for ...

I will accomplish ...

I need to work on ...

Notes

WHAT I LIKED

WHAT I DID NOT LIKE

<table>
<tr><td>DATE</td><td>TIME</td></tr>
<tr><td>LOCATION</td><td>DURATION</td></tr>
<tr><td>METHOD</td><td>MANTRA</td></tr>
</table>

MEDITATION POSITION

MEDITATION FOCUS

THOUGHTS & INSIGHTS

MOOD WHEEL

QUALITY AND INTENSITY

FOCUS AND BREATHING

1 — 2 — 3 — 4 — 5 — 6 — 7 — 8 — 9 — 10

VISIONS AND EMOTIONS

REFLECTIONS

I am grateful for ...

I will accomplish ...

I need to work on ...

Notes

WHAT I LIKED

WHAT I DID NOT LIKE

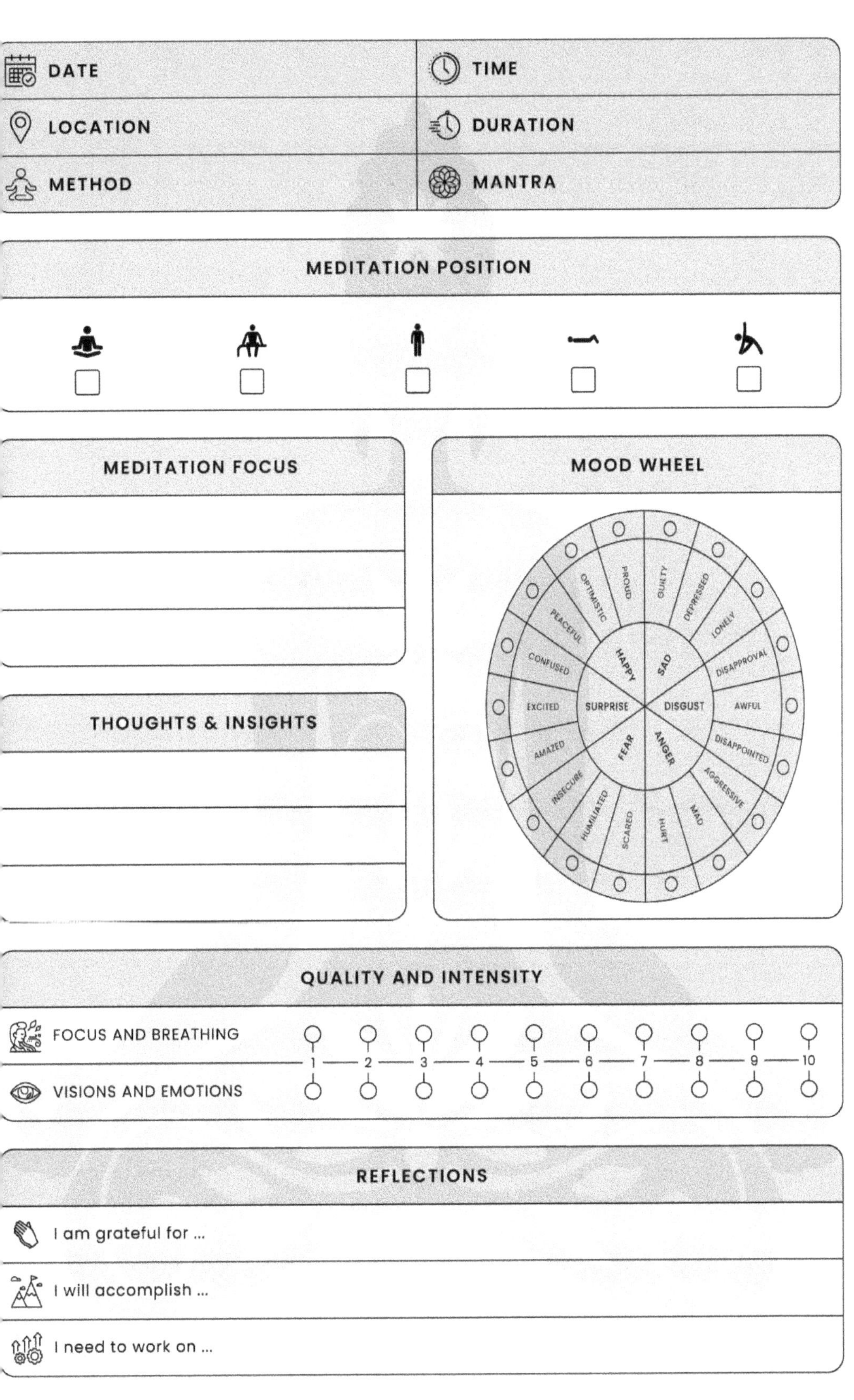

DATE	TIME
LOCATION	DURATION
METHOD	MANTRA

MEDITATION POSITION

☐ ☐ ☐ ☐ ☐

MEDITATION FOCUS

THOUGHTS & INSIGHTS

MOOD WHEEL

QUALITY AND INTENSITY

FOCUS AND BREATHING

1 — 2 — 3 — 4 — 5 — 6 — 7 — 8 — 9 — 10

VISIONS AND EMOTIONS

REFLECTIONS

I am grateful for ...

I will accomplish ...

I need to work on ...

Notes

WHAT I LIKED

WHAT I DID NOT LIKE

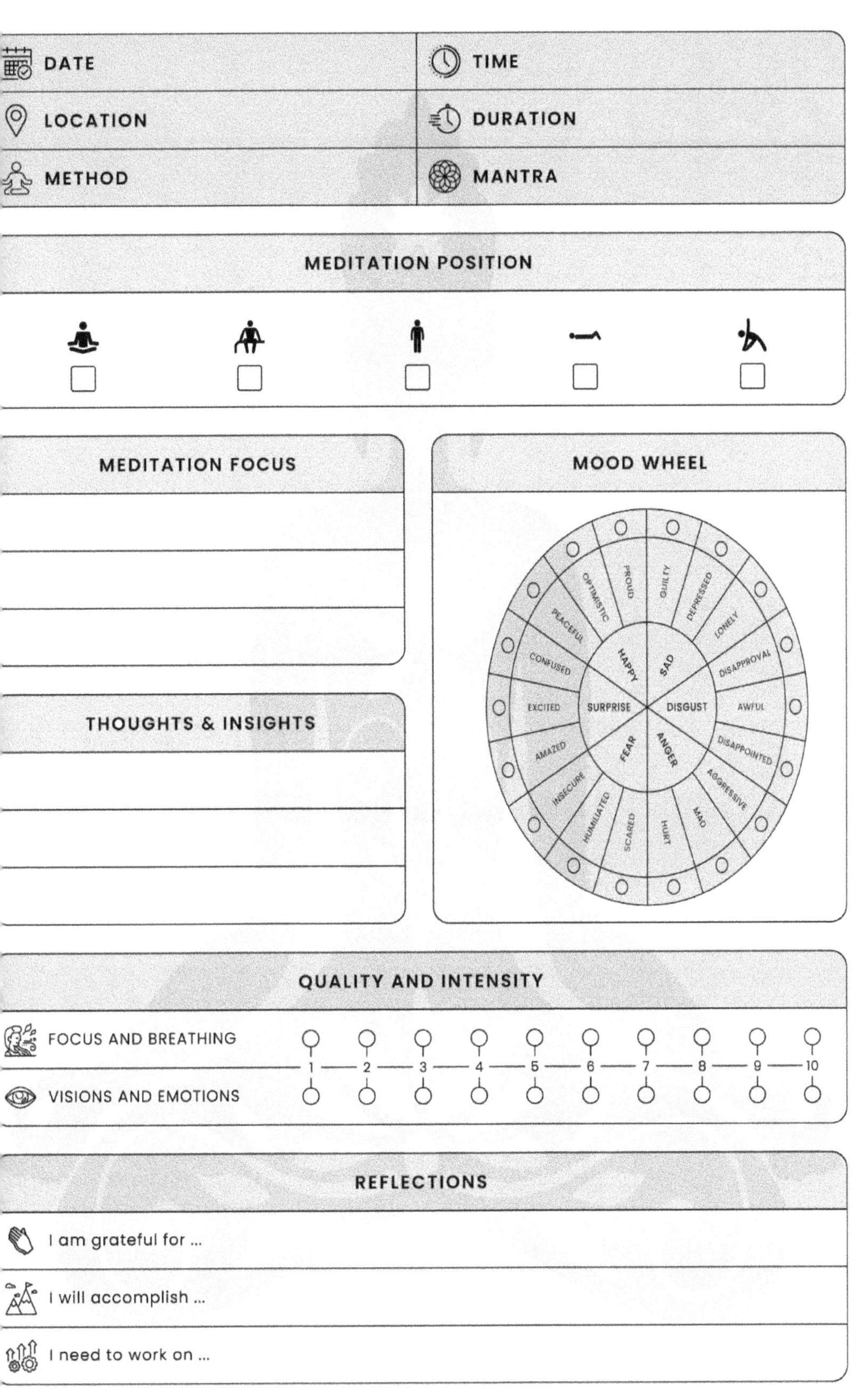

Notes

WHAT I LIKED

____

____

____

____

WHAT I DID NOT LIKE

____

____

____

____

DATE

TIME

LOCATION

DURATION

METHOD

MANTRA

MEDITATION POSITION

☐ ☐ ☐ ☐ ☐

MEDITATION FOCUS

MOOD WHEEL

THOUGHTS & INSIGHTS

QUALITY AND INTENSITY

FOCUS AND BREATHING

1 — 2 — 3 — 4 — 5 — 6 — 7 — 8 — 9 — 10

VISIONS AND EMOTIONS

REFLECTIONS

I am grateful for ...

I will accomplish ...

I need to work on ...

Notes

WHAT I LIKED

WHAT I DID NOT LIKE

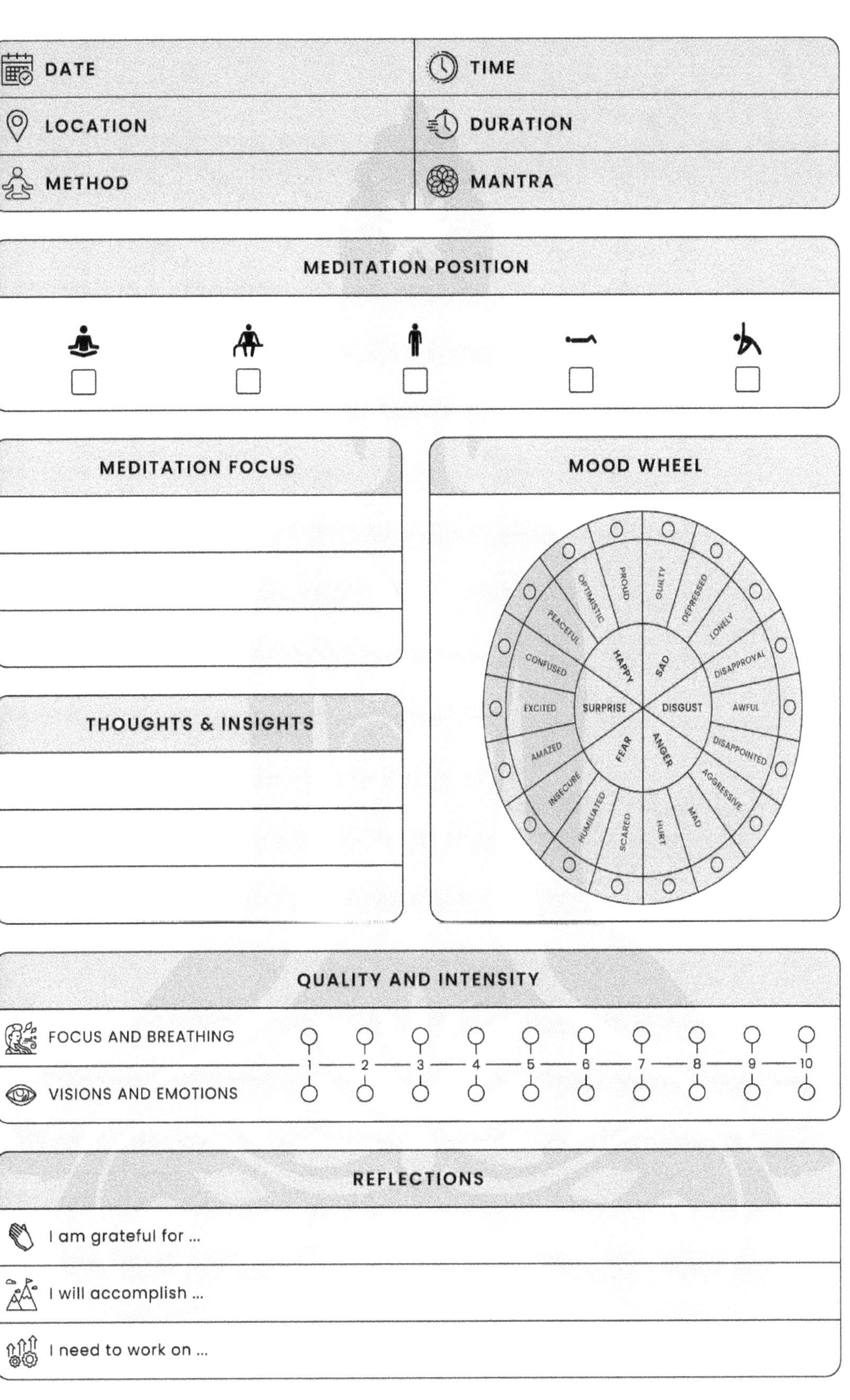

DATE
TIME
LOCATION
DURATION
METHOD
MANTRA
MEDITATION POSITION
MEDITATION FOCUS
MOOD WHEEL
OPTIMISTIC
PROUD
GUILTY
DEPRESSED
PEACEFUL
LONELY
CONFUSED
HAPPY
SAD
DISAPPROVAL
EXCITED
SURPRISE
DISGUST
AWFUL
AMAZED
FEAR
ANGER
DISAPPOINTED
INSECURE
AGGRESSIVE
HUMILIATED
SCARED
HURT
MAD
THOUGHTS & INSIGHTS
QUALITY AND INTENSITY
FOCUS AND BREATHING
1 2 3 4 5 6 7 8 9 10
VISIONS AND EMOTIONS
REFLECTIONS
I am grateful for ...
I will accomplish ...
I need to work on ...

Notes

WHAT I LIKED

WHAT I DID NOT LIKE

MEDITATION JOURNAL

DATE	TIME
LOCATION	DURATION
METHOD	MANTRA

MEDITATION POSITION

☐ ☐ ☐ ☐ ☐

MEDITATION FOCUS

MOOD WHEEL

THOUGHTS & INSIGHTS

QUALITY AND INTENSITY

FOCUS AND BREATHING

1 — 2 — 3 — 4 — 5 — 6 — 7 — 8 — 9 — 10

VISIONS AND EMOTIONS

REFLECTIONS

I am grateful for ...

I will accomplish ...

I need to work on ...

Notes

WHAT I LIKED

WHAT I DID NOT LIKE

MEDITATION POSITION

MEDITATION FOCUS

THOUGHTS & INSIGHTS

MOOD WHEEL

QUALITY AND INTENSITY

FOCUS AND BREATHING

1 — 2 — 3 — 4 — 5 — 6 — 7 — 8 — 9 — 10

VISIONS AND EMOTIONS

REFLECTIONS

I am grateful for ...

I will accomplish ...

I need to work on ...

Notes

WHAT I LIKED

WHAT I DID NOT LIKE

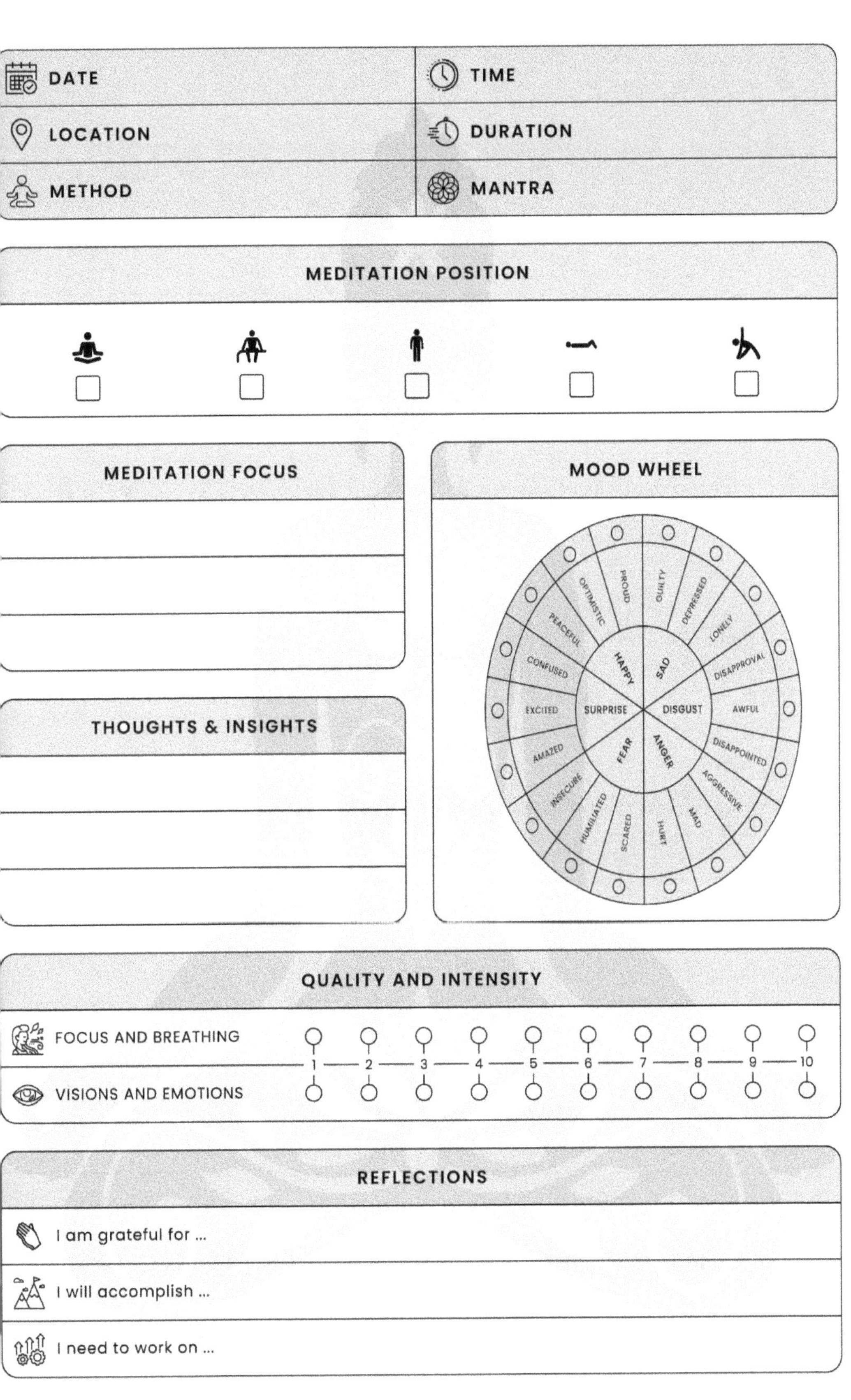

DATE	TIME
LOCATION	DURATION
METHOD	MANTRA

MEDITATION POSITION

☐ ☐ ☐ ☐ ☐

MEDITATION FOCUS

MOOD WHEEL

THOUGHTS & INSIGHTS

QUALITY AND INTENSITY

FOCUS AND BREATHING

1 — 2 — 3 — 4 — 5 — 6 — 7 — 8 — 9 — 10

VISIONS AND EMOTIONS

REFLECTIONS

I am grateful for …

I will accomplish …

I need to work on …

Notes

WHAT I LIKED

WHAT I DID NOT LIKE

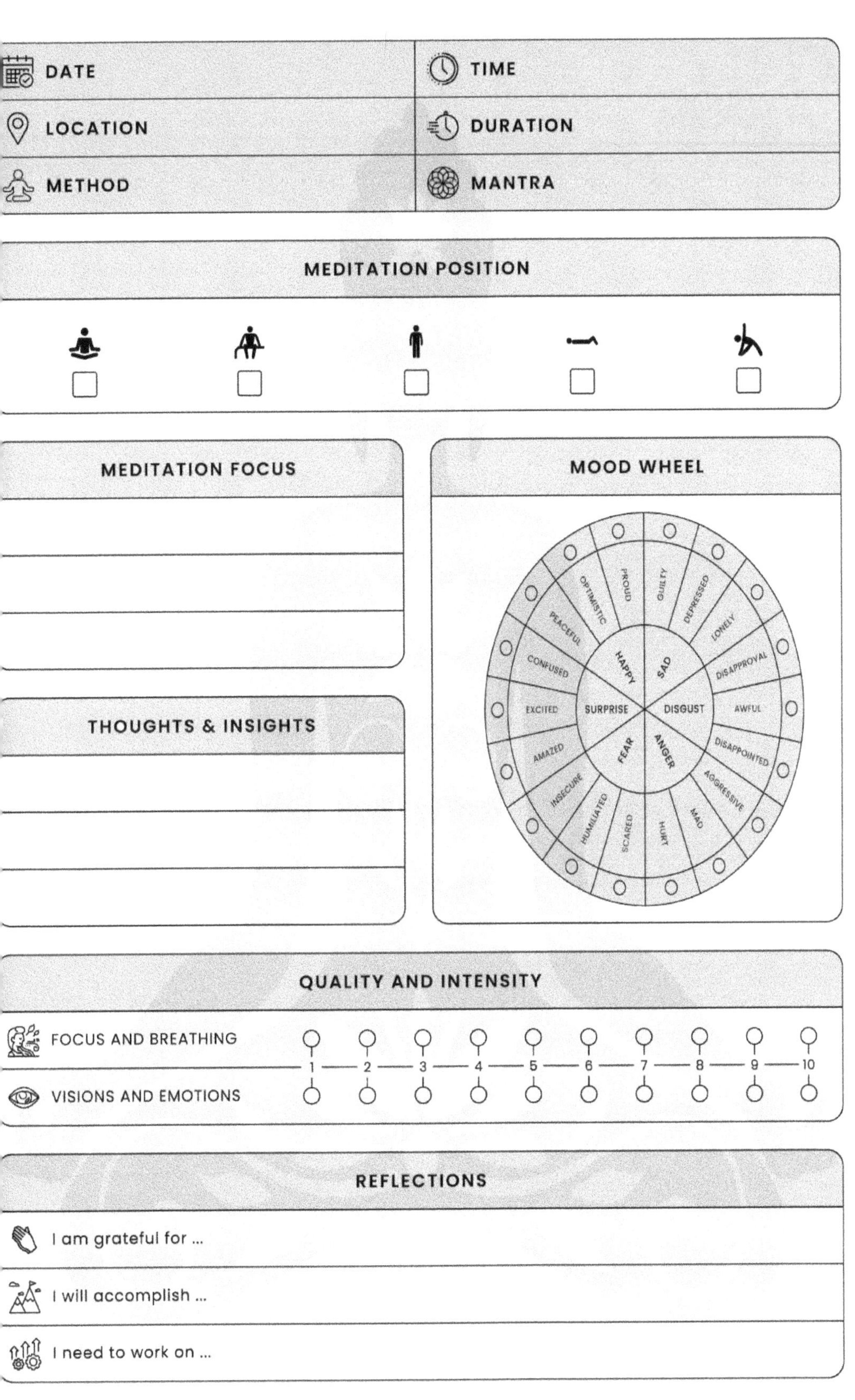

DATE
TIME
LOCATION
DURATION
METHOD
MANTRA

MEDITATION POSITION

MEDITATION FOCUS

MOOD WHEEL

OPTIMISTIC
PROUD
GUILTY
DEPRESSED
PEACEFUL
LONELY
CONFUSED
HAPPY
SAD
DISAPPROVAL
EXCITED
SURPRISE
DISGUST
AWFUL
AMAZED
FEAR
ANGER
DISAPPOINTED
INSECURE
AGGRESSIVE
HUMILIATED
SCARED
HURT
MAD

THOUGHTS & INSIGHTS

QUALITY AND INTENSITY

FOCUS AND BREATHING
1 — 2 — 3 — 4 — 5 — 6 — 7 — 8 — 9 — 10
VISIONS AND EMOTIONS

REFLECTIONS

I am grateful for ...

I will accomplish ...

I need to work on ...

Notes

WHAT I LIKED

WHAT I DID NOT LIKE

MEDITATION POSITION

MEDITATION FOCUS

THOUGHTS & INSIGHTS

MOOD WHEEL

QUALITY AND INTENSITY

FOCUS AND BREATHING

1 — 2 — 3 — 4 — 5 — 6 — 7 — 8 — 9 — 10

VISIONS AND EMOTIONS

REFLECTIONS

I am grateful for ...

I will accomplish ...

I need to work on ...

Notes

WHAT I LIKED

WHAT I DID NOT LIKE

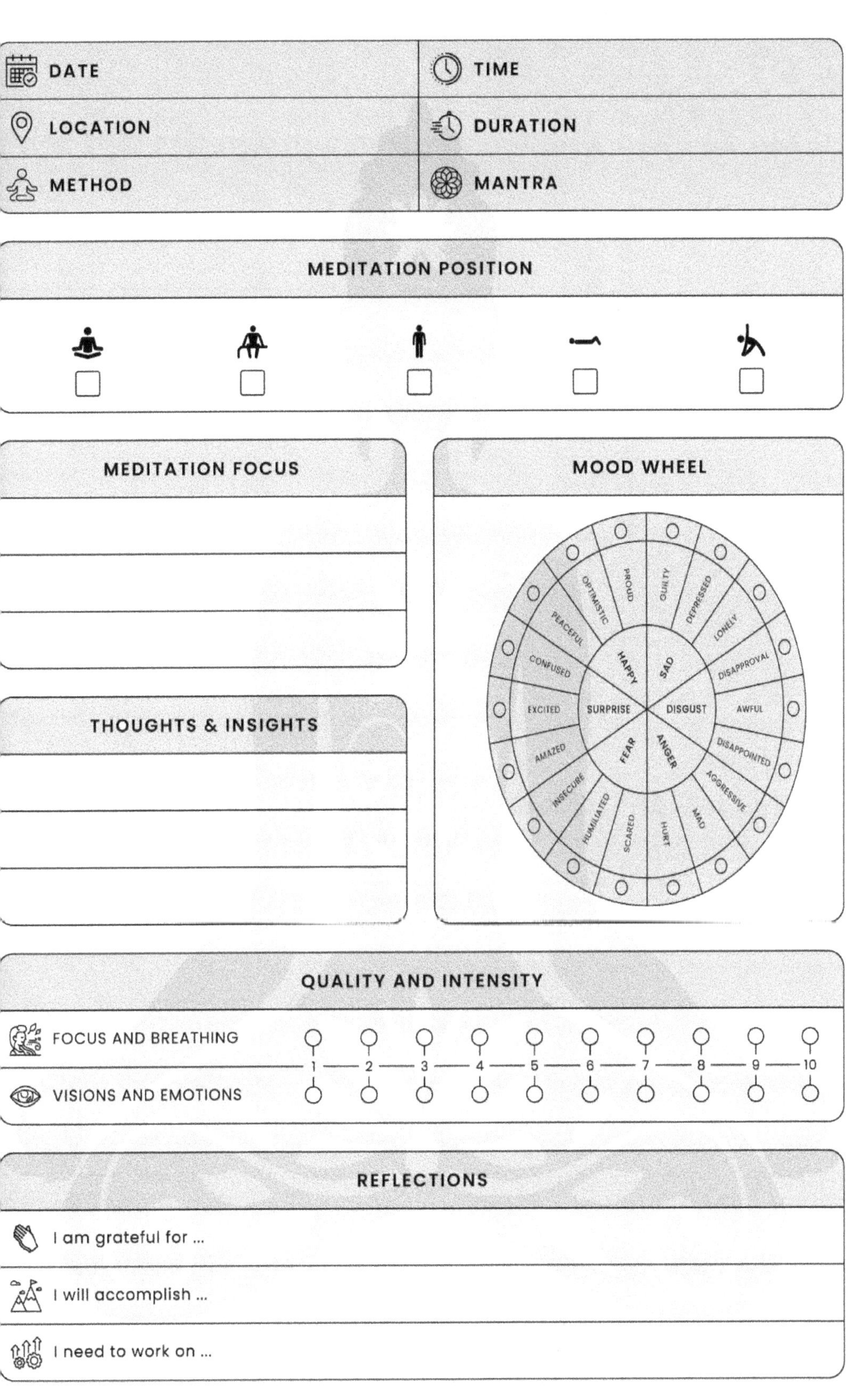

DATE
TIME
LOCATION
DURATION
METHOD
MANTRA

MEDITATION POSITION

MEDITATION FOCUS

MOOD WHEEL

OPTIMISTIC
PROUD
GUILTY
DEPRESSED
PEACEFUL
LONELY
CONFUSED
DISAPPROVAL
HAPPY
SAD
EXCITED
SURPRISE
DISGUST
AWFUL
AMAZED
FEAR
ANGER
DISAPPOINTED
INSECURE
AGGRESSIVE
HUMILIATED
SCARED
HURT
MAD

THOUGHTS & INSIGHTS

QUALITY AND INTENSITY

FOCUS AND BREATHING
1 2 3 4 5 6 7 8 9 10
VISIONS AND EMOTIONS

REFLECTIONS

I am grateful for ...

I will accomplish ...

I need to work on ...

Notes

WHAT I LIKED

WHAT I DID NOT LIKE

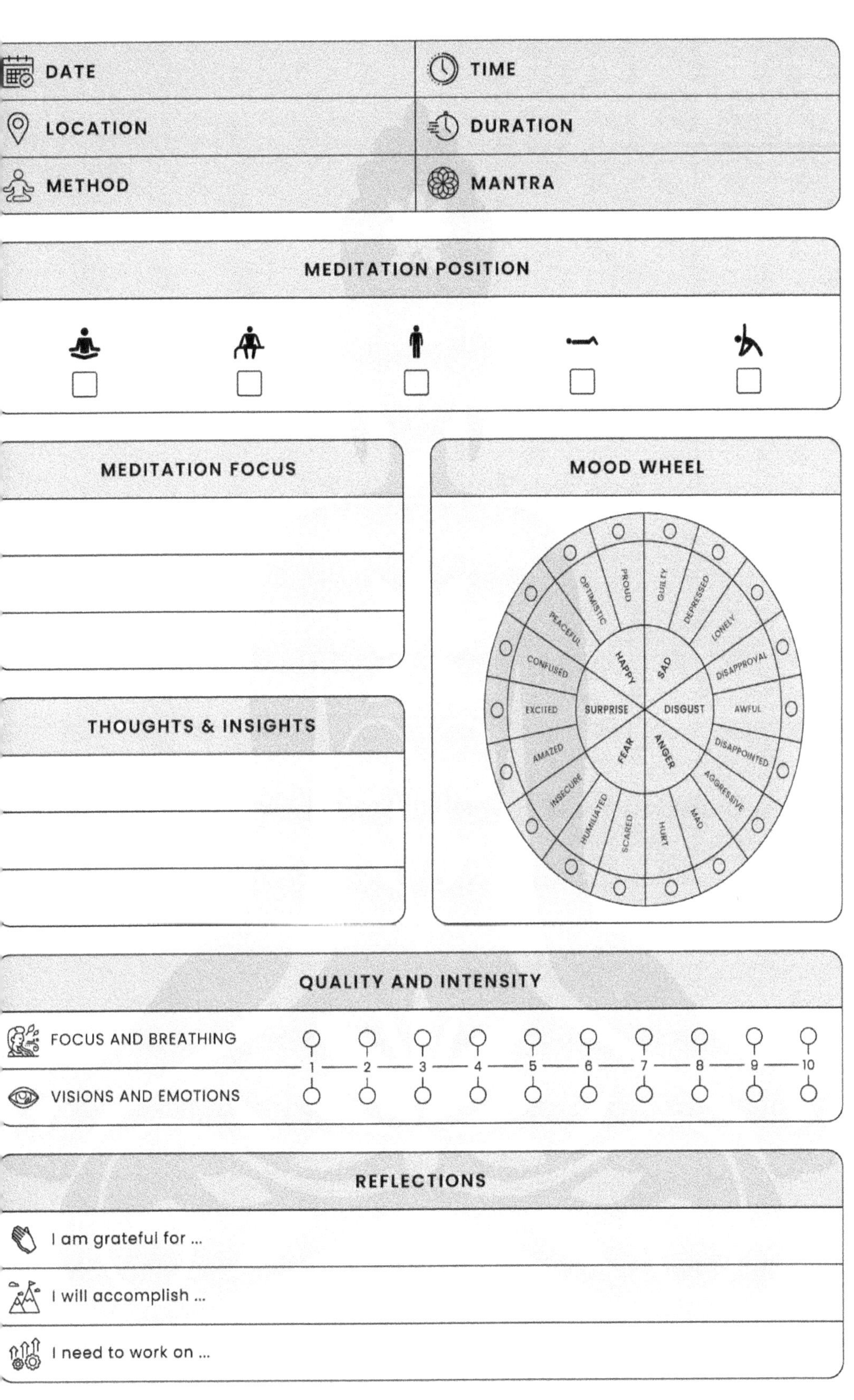
DATE
TIME
LOCATION
DURATION
METHOD
MANTRA

MEDITATION POSITION

MEDITATION FOCUS

MOOD WHEEL

OPTIMISTIC
PROUD
GUILTY
DEPRESSED
PEACEFUL
LONELY
CONFUSED
HAPPY
SAD
DISAPPROVAL
EXCITED
SURPRISE
DISGUST
AWFUL
AMAZED
FEAR
ANGER
DISAPPOINTED
INSECURE
AGGRESSIVE
HUMILIATED
SCARED
HURT
MAD

THOUGHTS & INSIGHTS

QUALITY AND INTENSITY

FOCUS AND BREATHING
1 — 2 — 3 — 4 — 5 — 6 — 7 — 8 — 9 — 10
VISIONS AND EMOTIONS

REFLECTIONS

I am grateful for ...

I will accomplish ...

I need to work on ...

Notes

WHAT I LIKED

WHAT I DID NOT LIKE

DATE	TIME
LOCATION	DURATION
METHOD	MANTRA

MEDITATION POSITION

☐ ☐ ☐ ☐ ☐

MEDITATION FOCUS

THOUGHTS & INSIGHTS

MOOD WHEEL

QUALITY AND INTENSITY

FOCUS AND BREATHING

1 — 2 — 3 — 4 — 5 — 6 — 7 — 8 — 9 — 10

VISIONS AND EMOTIONS

REFLECTIONS

I am grateful for ...

I will accomplish ...

I need to work on ...

Notes

WHAT I LIKED

WHAT I DID NOT LIKE

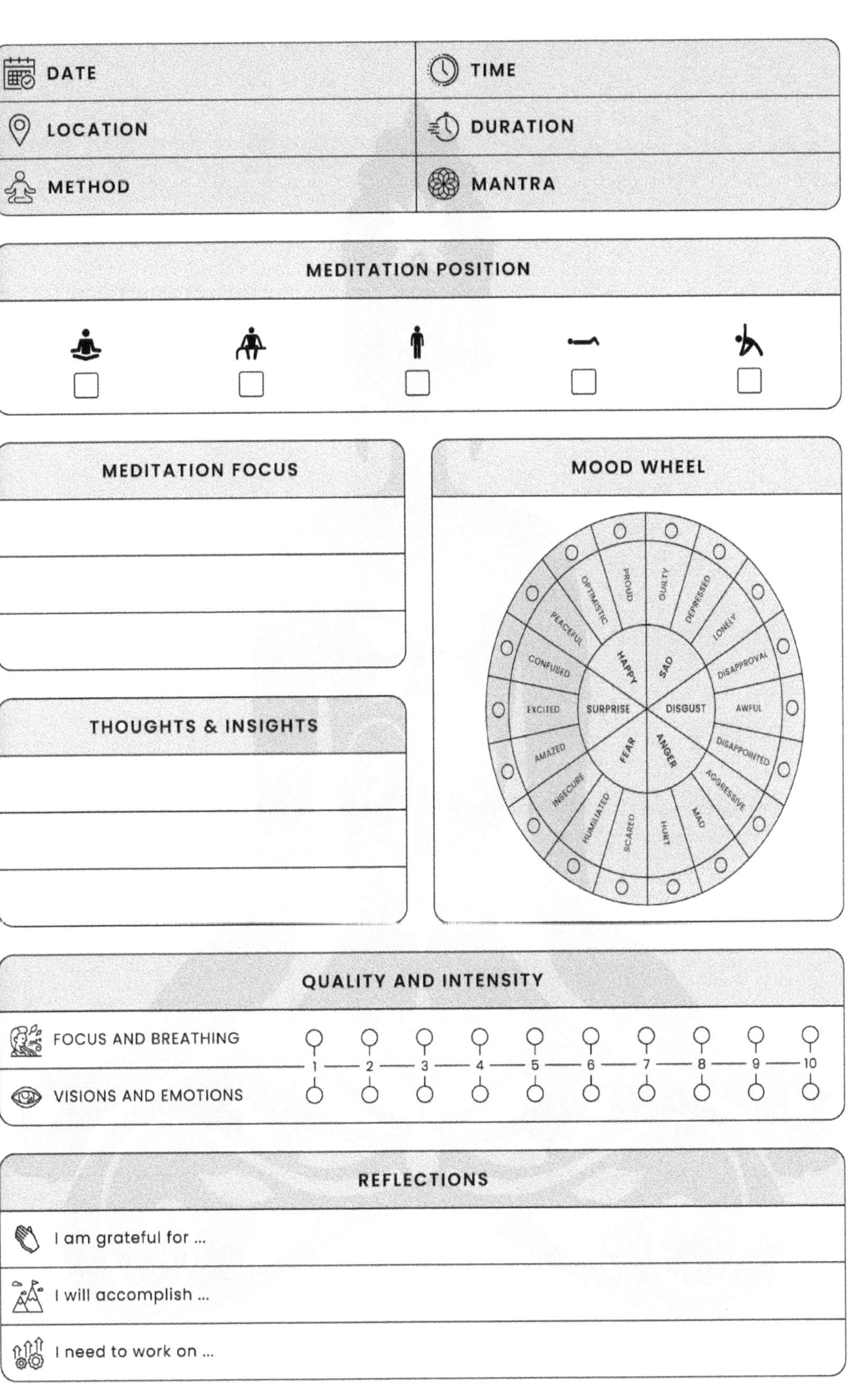

DATE
TIME
LOCATION
DURATION
METHOD
MANTRA

MEDITATION POSITION

MEDITATION FOCUS

MOOD WHEEL

OPTIMISTIC
PROUD
GUILTY
DEPRESSED
PEACEFUL
LONELY
CONFUSED
DISAPPROVAL
HAPPY
SAD
EXCITED
SURPRISE
DISGUST
AWFUL
AMAZED
FEAR
ANGER
DISAPPOINTED
INSECURE
AGGRESSIVE
HUMILIATED
SCARED
HURT
MAD

THOUGHTS & INSIGHTS

QUALITY AND INTENSITY

FOCUS AND BREATHING
1 — 2 — 3 — 4 — 5 — 6 — 7 — 8 — 9 — 10
VISIONS AND EMOTIONS

REFLECTIONS

I am grateful for ...

I will accomplish ...

I need to work on ...

Notes

WHAT I LIKED

WHAT I DID NOT LIKE

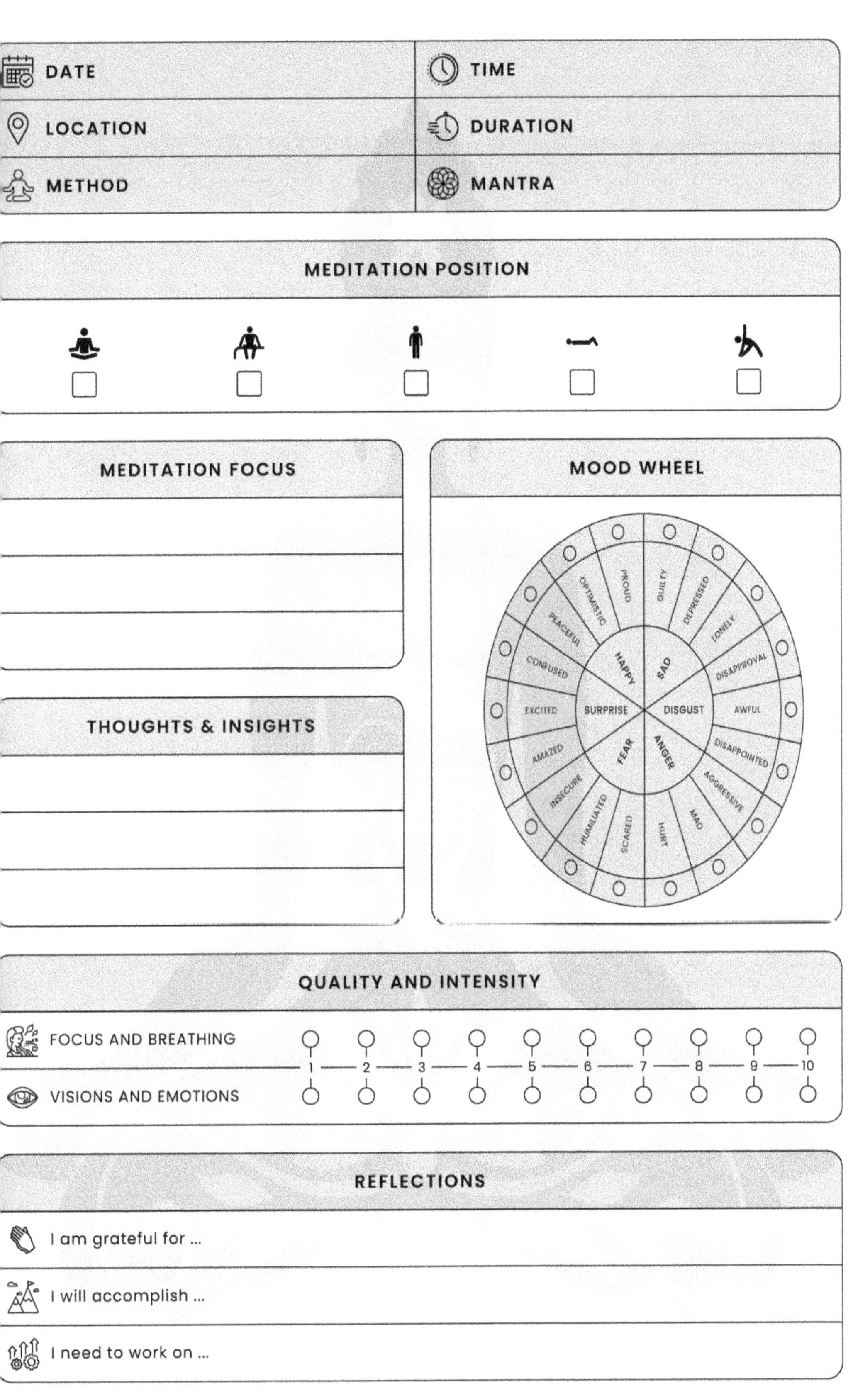

DATE
TIME
LOCATION
DURATION
METHOD
MANTRA
MEDITATION POSITION
MEDITATION FOCUS
MOOD WHEEL
HAPPY
SAD
SURPRISE
DISGUST
FEAR
ANGER
OPTIMISTIC
PROUD
GUILTY
DEPRESSED
PEACEFUL
LONELY
CONFUSED
DISAPPROVAL
EXCITED
AWFUL
AMAZED
DISAPPOINTED
INSECURE
AGGRESSIVE
HUMILIATED
MAD
SCARED
HURT
THOUGHTS & INSIGHTS
QUALITY AND INTENSITY
FOCUS AND BREATHING
1 2 3 4 5 6 7 8 9 10
VISIONS AND EMOTIONS
REFLECTIONS
I am grateful for ...
I will accomplish ...
I need to work on ...

Notes

WHAT I LIKED

WHAT I DID NOT LIKE

MEDITATION POSITION

MEDITATION FOCUS

MOOD WHEEL

THOUGHTS & INSIGHTS

QUALITY AND INTENSITY

FOCUS AND BREATHING

1 — 2 — 3 — 4 — 5 — 6 — 7 — 8 — 9 — 10

VISIONS AND EMOTIONS

REFLECTIONS

I am grateful for ...

I will accomplish ...

I need to work on ...

Notes

WHAT I LIKED

WHAT I DID NOT LIKE

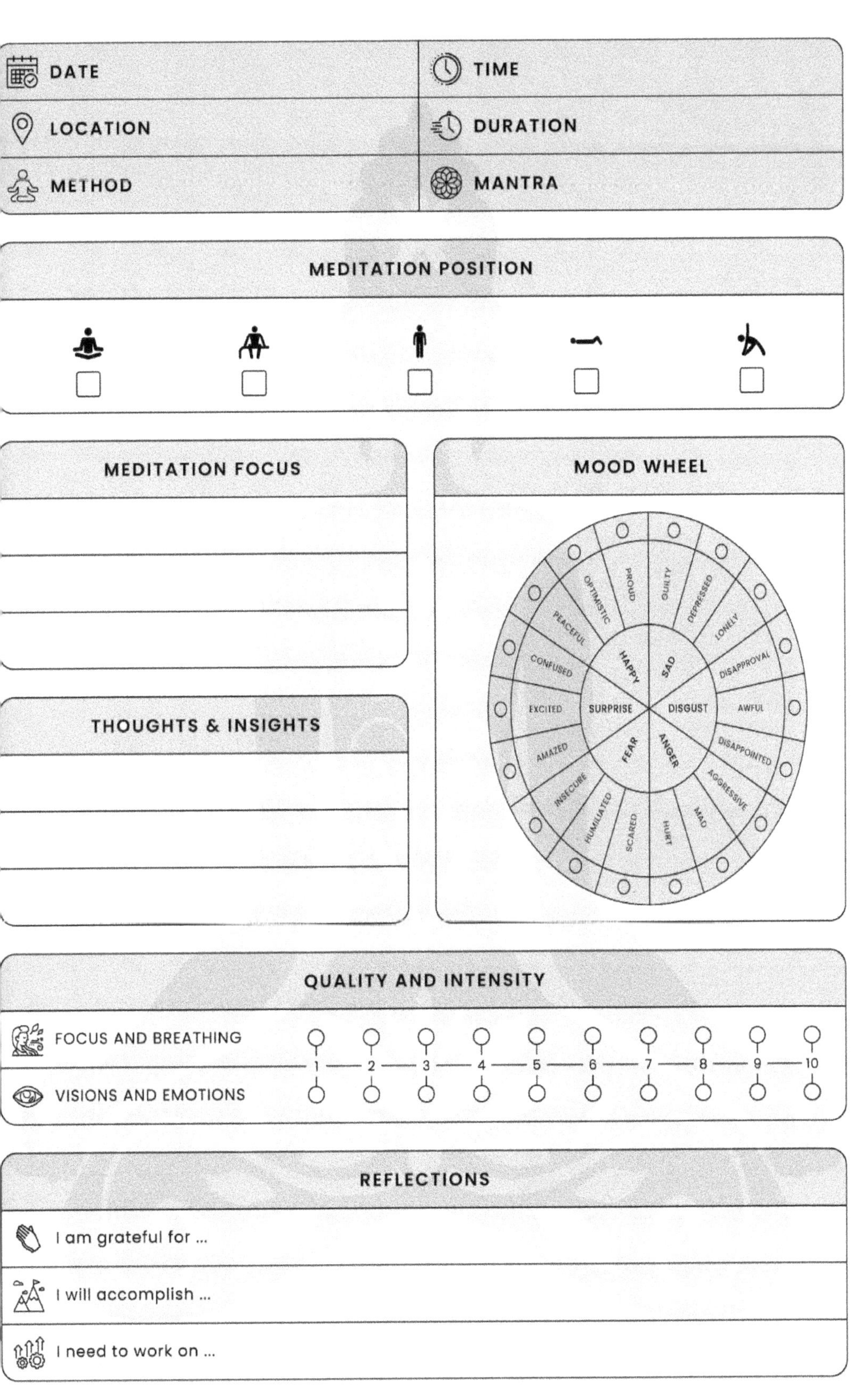

DATE
TIME
LOCATION
DURATION
METHOD
MANTRA

MEDITATION POSITION

MEDITATION FOCUS

MOOD WHEEL

OPTIMISTIC
PROUD
GUILTY
DEPRESSED
PEACEFUL
LONELY
CONFUSED
DISAPPROVAL
HAPPY
SAD
EXCITED
SURPRISE
DISGUST
AWFUL
AMAZED
FEAR
ANGER
DISAPPOINTED
INSECURE
AGGRESSIVE
HUMILIATED
SCARED
HURT
MAD

THOUGHTS & INSIGHTS

QUALITY AND INTENSITY

FOCUS AND BREATHING
1 — 2 — 3 — 4 — 5 — 6 — 7 — 8 — 9 — 10
VISIONS AND EMOTIONS

REFLECTIONS

I am grateful for ...

I will accomplish ...

I need to work on ...

Notes

WHAT I LIKED

WHAT I DID NOT LIKE

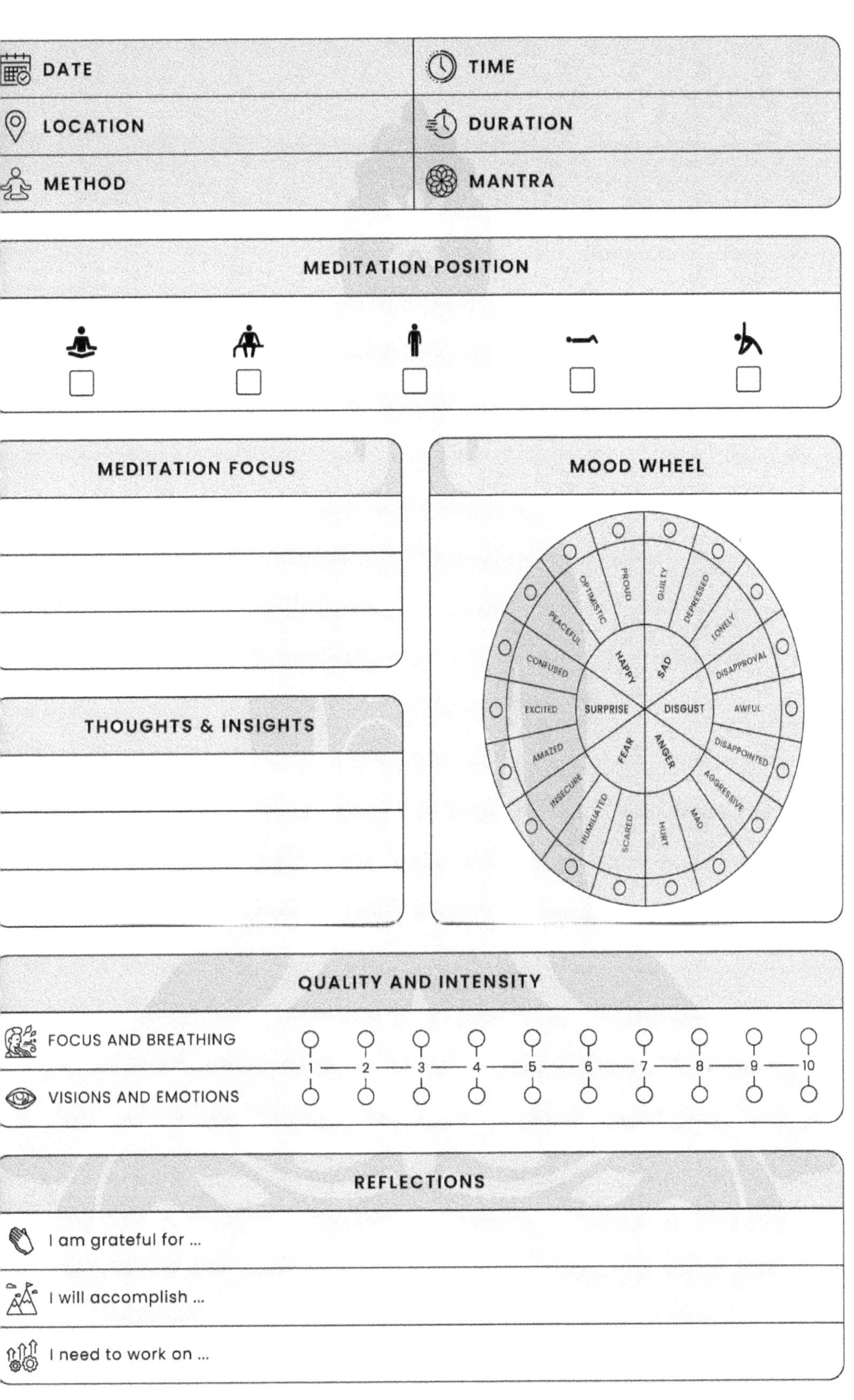

DATE
TIME
LOCATION
DURATION
METHOD
MANTRA
MEDITATION POSITION
MEDITATION FOCUS
MOOD WHEEL
OPTIMISTIC
PROUD
GUILTY
DEPRESSED
PEACEFUL
LONELY
CONFUSED
HAPPY
SAD
DISAPPROVAL
EXCITED
SURPRISE
DISGUST
AWFUL
AMAZED
FEAR
ANGER
DISAPPOINTED
INSECURE
AGGRESSIVE
HUMILIATED
SCARED
HURT
MAD
THOUGHTS & INSIGHTS
QUALITY AND INTENSITY
FOCUS AND BREATHING
1
2
3
4
5
6
7
8
9
10
VISIONS AND EMOTIONS
REFLECTIONS
I am grateful for ...
I will accomplish ...
I need to work on ...

Notes

WHAT I LIKED

WHAT I DID NOT LIKE

MEDITATION POSITION

MEDITATION FOCUS

THOUGHTS & INSIGHTS

MOOD WHEEL

QUALITY AND INTENSITY

FOCUS AND BREATHING

VISIONS AND EMOTIONS

1 — 2 — 3 — 4 — 5 — 6 — 7 — 8 — 9 — 10

REFLECTIONS

I am grateful for ...

I will accomplish ...

I need to work on ...

Notes

WHAT I LIKED

____

____

____

____

WHAT I DID NOT LIKE

____

____

____

____

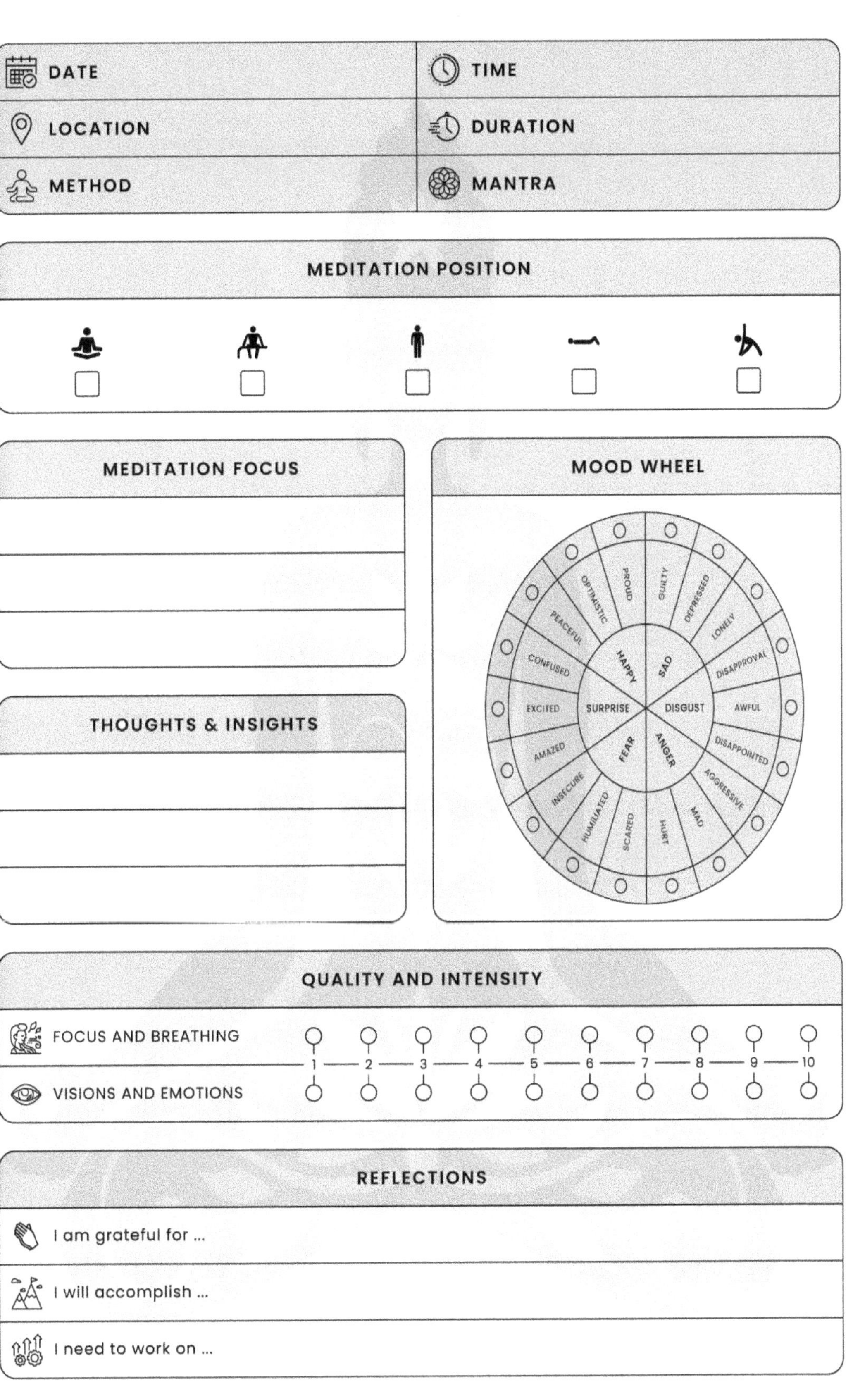

DATE
TIME
LOCATION
DURATION
METHOD
MANTRA

MEDITATION POSITION

MEDITATION FOCUS

MOOD WHEEL

OPTIMISTIC
PROUD
GUILTY
DEPRESSED
PEACEFUL
LONELY
CONFUSED
DISAPPROVAL
HAPPY
SAD
EXCITED
SURPRISE
DISGUST
AWFUL
AMAZED
FEAR
ANGER
DISAPPOINTED
INSECURE
AGGRESSIVE
HUMILIATED
SCARED
HURT
MAD

THOUGHTS & INSIGHTS

QUALITY AND INTENSITY

FOCUS AND BREATHING
1 — 2 — 3 — 4 — 5 — 6 — 7 — 8 — 9 — 10
VISIONS AND EMOTIONS

REFLECTIONS

I am grateful for ...

I will accomplish ...

I need to work on ...

Notes

WHAT I LIKED

WHAT I DID NOT LIKE

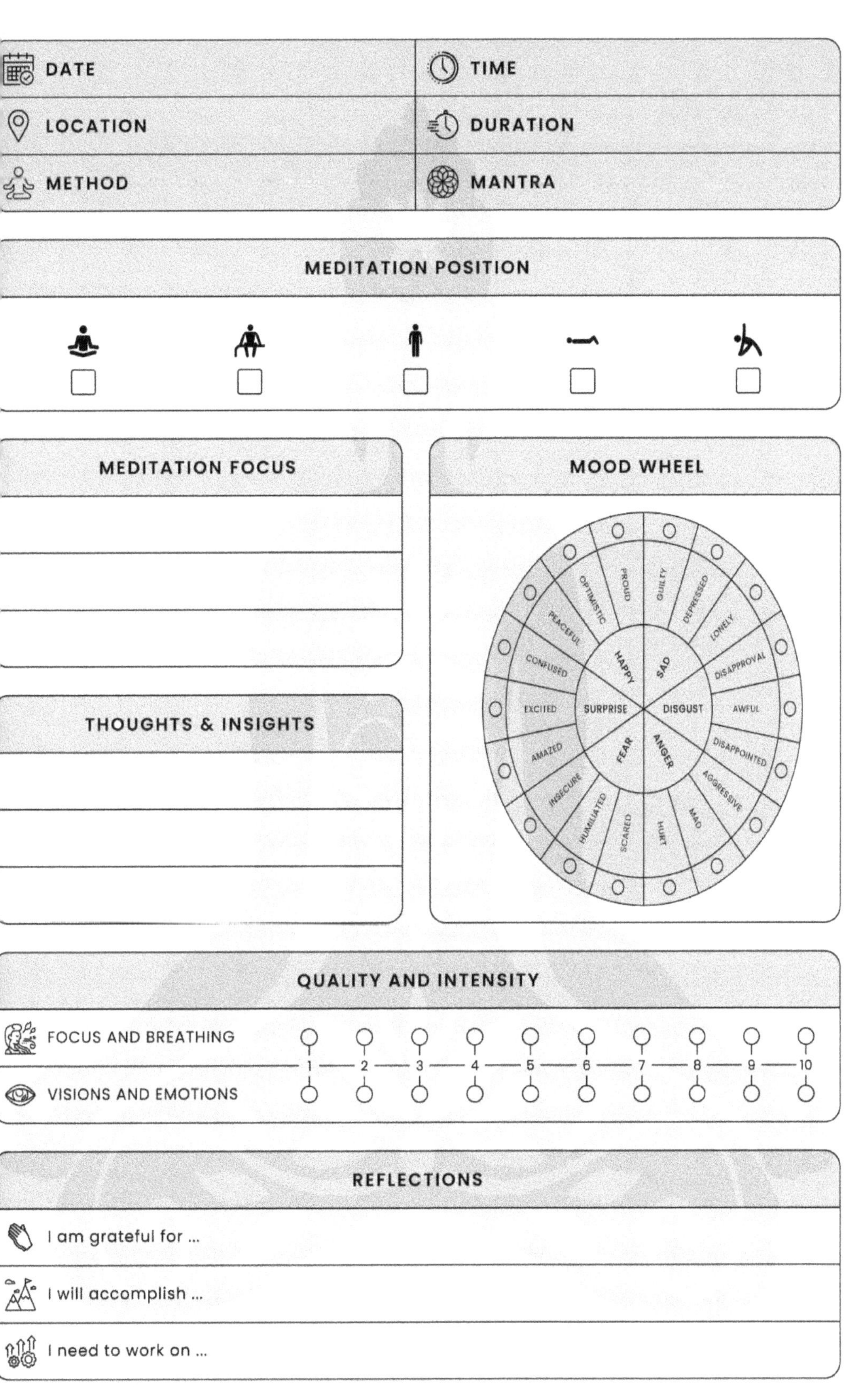

DATE
TIME
LOCATION
DURATION
METHOD
MANTRA

MEDITATION POSITION

MEDITATION FOCUS

MOOD WHEEL

OPTIMISTIC
PROUD
GUILTY
DEPRESSED
PEACEFUL
LONELY
CONFUSED
HAPPY
SAD
DISAPPROVAL
EXCITED
SURPRISE
DISGUST
AWFUL
AMAZED
FEAR
ANGER
DISAPPOINTED
INSECURE
AGGRESSIVE
HUMILIATED
SCARED
HURT
MAD

THOUGHTS & INSIGHTS

QUALITY AND INTENSITY

FOCUS AND BREATHING
1 — 2 — 3 — 4 — 5 — 6 — 7 — 8 — 9 — 10
VISIONS AND EMOTIONS

REFLECTIONS

I am grateful for ...

I will accomplish ...

I need to work on ...

Notes

WHAT I LIKED

WHAT I DID NOT LIKE

MEDITATION POSITION

MEDITATION FOCUS

THOUGHTS & INSIGHTS

MOOD WHEEL

QUALITY AND INTENSITY

FOCUS AND BREATHING

1 — 2 — 3 — 4 — 5 — 6 — 7 — 8 — 9 — 10

VISIONS AND EMOTIONS

REFLECTIONS

I am grateful for …

I will accomplish …

I need to work on …

Notes

WHAT I LIKED

WHAT I DID NOT LIKE

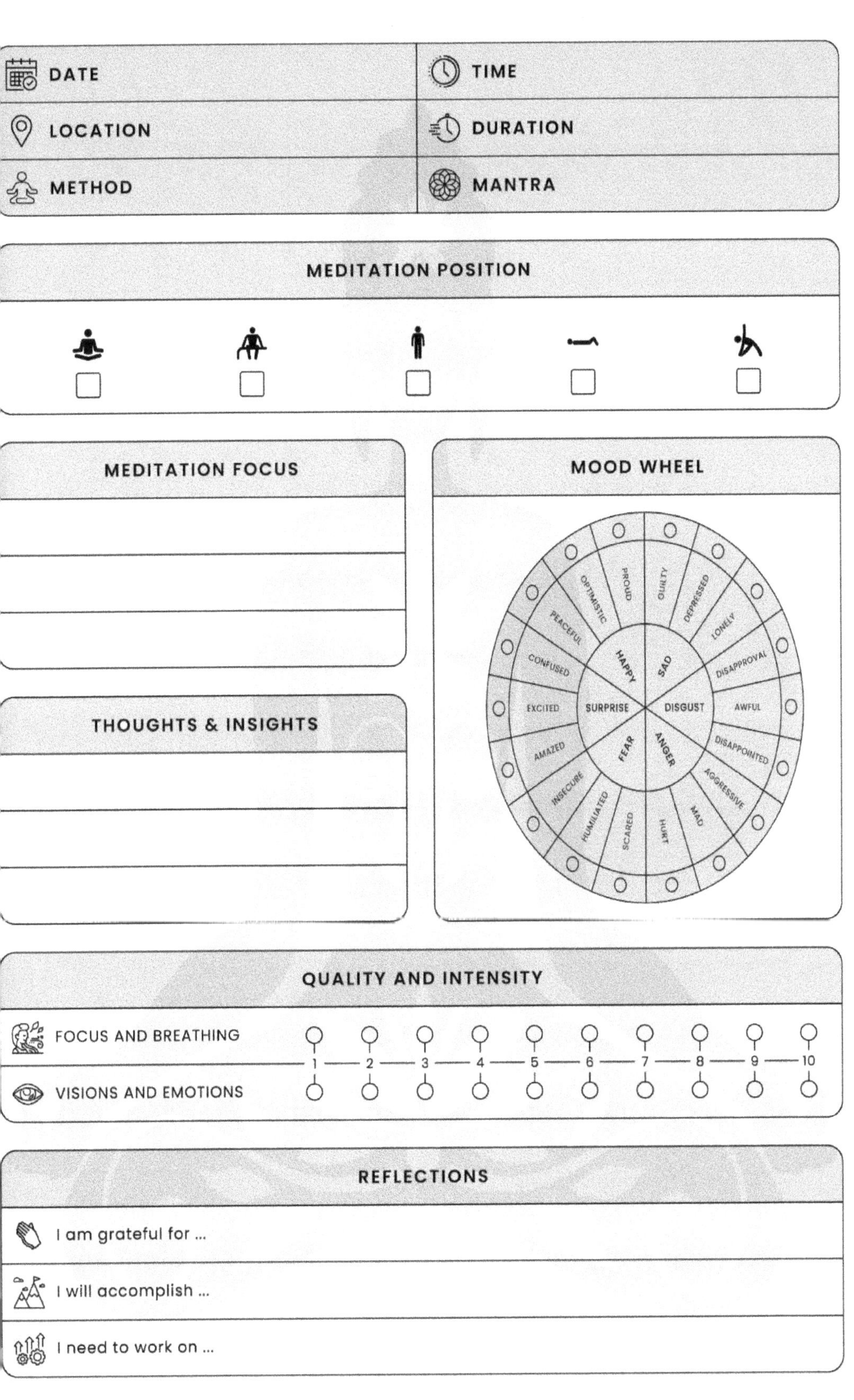

DATE
TIME
LOCATION
DURATION
METHOD
MANTRA

MEDITATION POSITION

MEDITATION FOCUS

MOOD WHEEL

OPTIMISTIC
PROUD
GUILTY
DEPRESSED
PEACEFUL
LONELY
CONFUSED
DISAPPROVAL
HAPPY
SAD
EXCITED
SURPRISE
DISGUST
AWFUL
AMAZED
FEAR
ANGER
DISAPPOINTED
INSECURE
AGGRESSIVE
HUMILIATED
SCARED
HURT
MAD

THOUGHTS & INSIGHTS

QUALITY AND INTENSITY

FOCUS AND BREATHING
1 — 2 — 3 — 4 — 5 — 6 — 7 — 8 — 9 — 10
VISIONS AND EMOTIONS

REFLECTIONS

I am grateful for ...

I will accomplish ...

I need to work on ...

Notes

WHAT I LIKED

WHAT I DID NOT LIKE

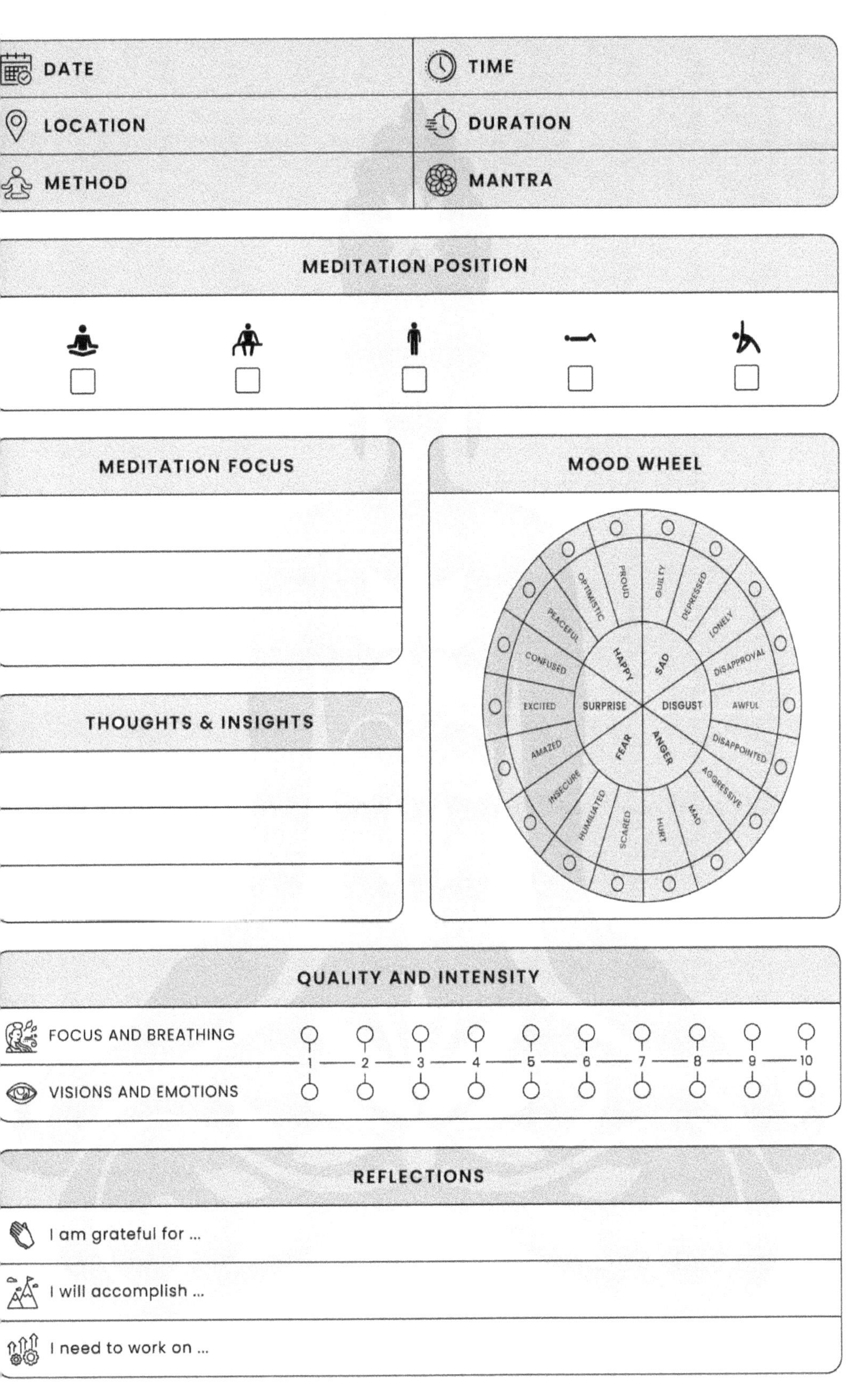

DATE
TIME
LOCATION
DURATION
METHOD
MANTRA

MEDITATION POSITION

MEDITATION FOCUS

MOOD WHEEL

OPTIMISTIC
PROUD
GUILTY
DEPRESSED
PEACEFUL
LONELY
CONFUSED
HAPPY
SAD
DISAPPROVAL
EXCITED
SURPRISE
DISGUST
AWFUL
AMAZED
FEAR
ANGER
DISAPPOINTED
INSECURE
AGGRESSIVE
HUMILIATED
SCARED
HURT
MAD

THOUGHTS & INSIGHTS

QUALITY AND INTENSITY

FOCUS AND BREATHING
1 — 2 — 3 — 4 — 5 — 6 — 7 — 8 — 9 — 10
VISIONS AND EMOTIONS

REFLECTIONS

I am grateful for ...

I will accomplish ...

I need to work on ...

Notes

WHAT I LIKED

WHAT I DID NOT LIKE

<table>
<tr><td>📅 DATE</td><td>🕐 TIME</td></tr>
<tr><td>📍 LOCATION</td><td>⏱ DURATION</td></tr>
<tr><td>🧘 METHOD</td><td>✳ MANTRA</td></tr>
</table>

MEDITATION POSITION

☐   ☐   ☐   ☐   ☐

MEDITATION FOCUS

THOUGHTS & INSIGHTS

MOOD WHEEL

QUALITY AND INTENSITY

🌿 FOCUS AND BREATHING

1 — 2 — 3 — 4 — 5 — 6 — 7 — 8 — 9 — 10

👁 VISIONS AND EMOTIONS

REFLECTIONS

✋ I am grateful for ...

⛰ I will accomplish ...

⚙ I need to work on ...

Notes

WHAT I LIKED

WHAT I DID NOT LIKE

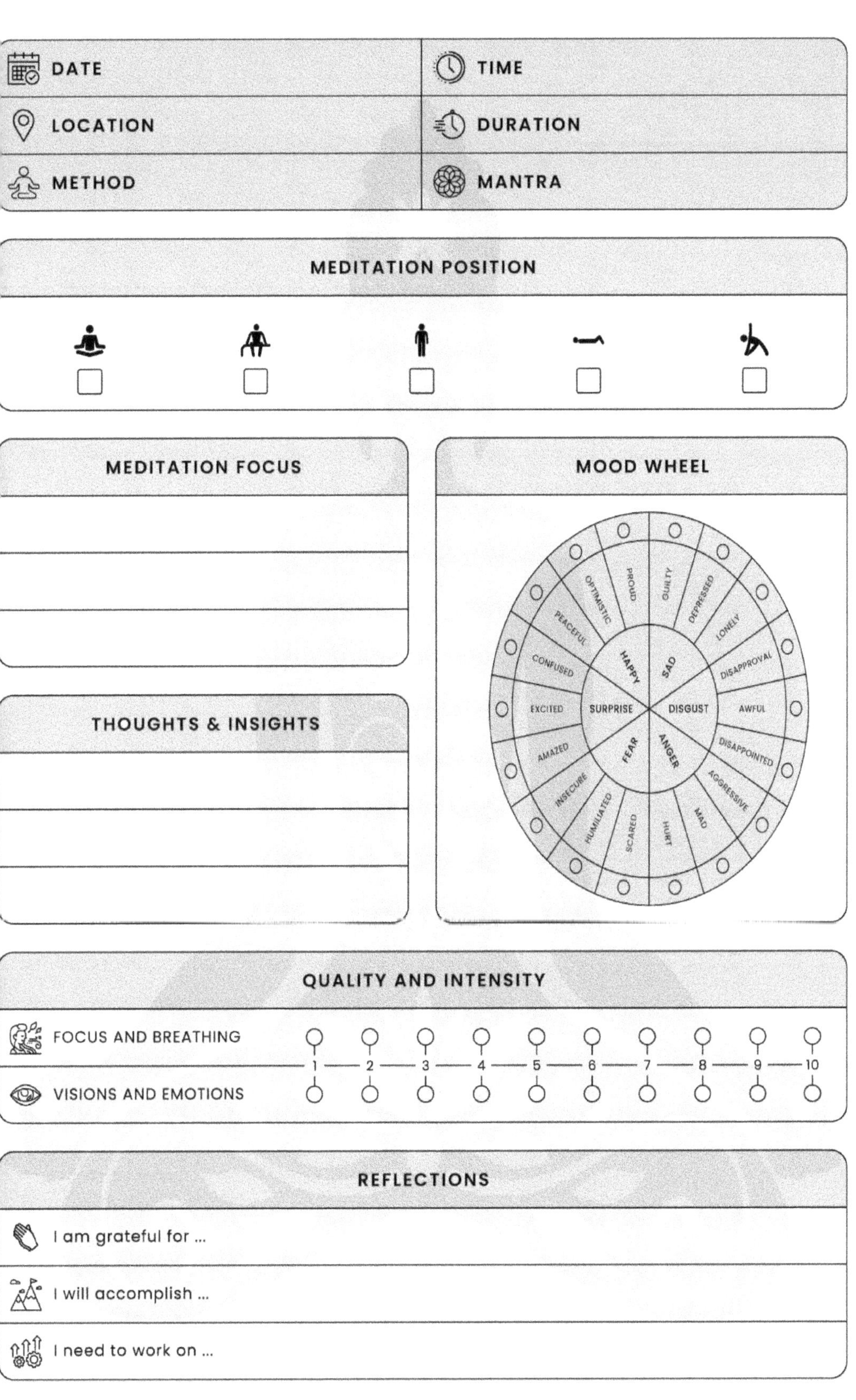

DATE	TIME
LOCATION	DURATION
METHOD	MANTRA

MEDITATION POSITION

MEDITATION FOCUS

THOUGHTS & INSIGHTS

MOOD WHEEL

QUALITY AND INTENSITY

FOCUS AND BREATHING

1 — 2 — 3 — 4 — 5 — 6 — 7 — 8 — 9 — 10

VISIONS AND EMOTIONS

REFLECTIONS

I am grateful for ...

I will accomplish ...

I need to work on ...

Notes

WHAT I LIKED

WHAT I DID NOT LIKE

MEDITATION POSITION

MEDITATION FOCUS

THOUGHTS & INSIGHTS

MOOD WHEEL

QUALITY AND INTENSITY

FOCUS AND BREATHING

1 — 2 — 3 — 4 — 5 — 6 — 7 — 8 — 9 — 10

VISIONS AND EMOTIONS

REFLECTIONS

I am grateful for ...

I will accomplish ...

I need to work on ...

Notes

WHAT I LIKED

WHAT I DID NOT LIKE

MEDITATION POSITION

MEDITATION FOCUS

MOOD WHEEL

THOUGHTS & INSIGHTS

QUALITY AND INTENSITY

FOCUS AND BREATHING

1 — 2 — 3 — 4 — 5 — 6 — 7 — 8 — 9 — 10

VISIONS AND EMOTIONS

REFLECTIONS

I am grateful for ...

I will accomplish ...

I need to work on ...

Notes

WHAT I LIKED

WHAT I DID NOT LIKE

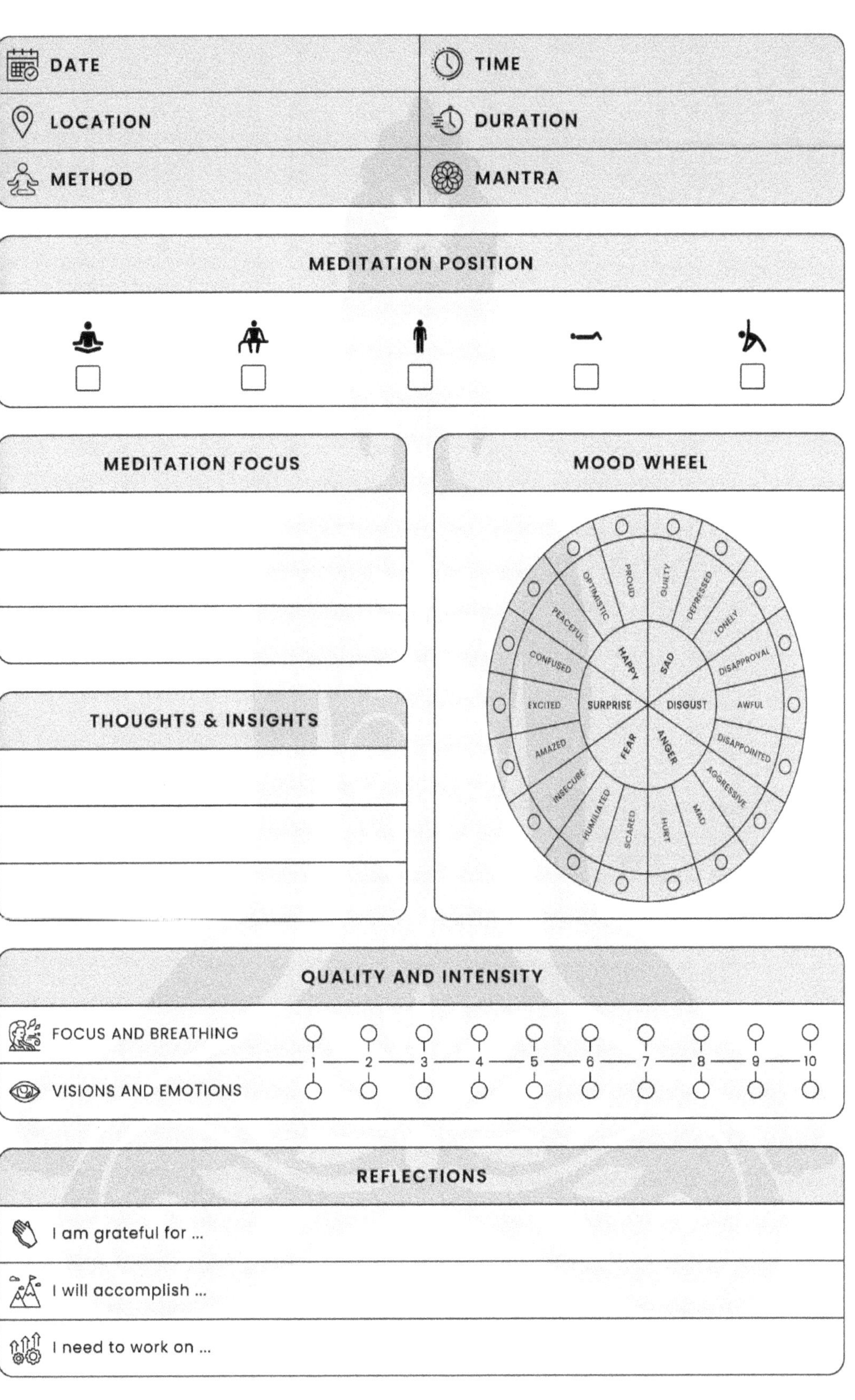

DATE
TIME
LOCATION
DURATION
METHOD
MANTRA
MEDITATION POSITION
MEDITATION FOCUS
MOOD WHEEL
OPTIMISTIC
PROUD
GUILTY
DEPRESSED
PEACEFUL
LONELY
CONFUSED
HAPPY
SAD
DISAPPROVAL
EXCITED
SURPRISE
DISGUST
AWFUL
AMAZED
FEAR
ANGER
DISAPPOINTED
INSECURE
AGGRESSIVE
HUMILIATED
SCARED
HURT
MAD
THOUGHTS & INSIGHTS
QUALITY AND INTENSITY
FOCUS AND BREATHING
1 — 2 — 3 — 4 — 5 — 6 — 7 — 8 — 9 — 10
VISIONS AND EMOTIONS
REFLECTIONS
I am grateful for ...
I will accomplish ...
I need to work on ...

Notes

WHAT I LIKED

WHAT I DID NOT LIKE

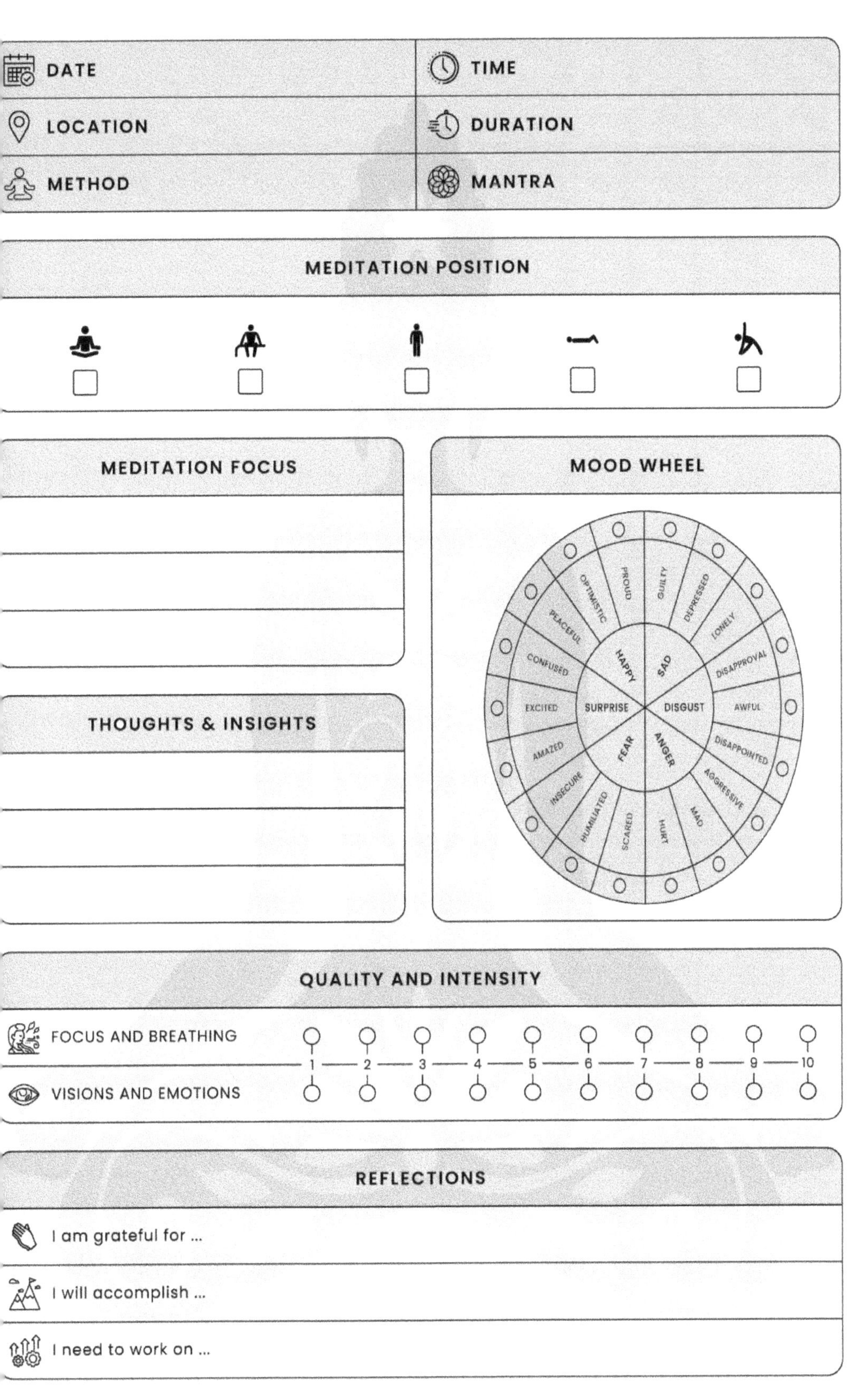

DATE
TIME
LOCATION
DURATION
METHOD
MANTRA
MEDITATION POSITION
MEDITATION FOCUS
MOOD WHEEL
OPTIMISTIC
PROUD
GUILTY
DEPRESSED
PEACEFUL
LONELY
CONFUSED
HAPPY
SAD
DISAPPROVAL
EXCITED
SURPRISE
DISGUST
AWFUL
AMAZED
FEAR
ANGER
DISAPPOINTED
INSECURE
AGGRESSIVE
HUMILIATED
SCARED
HURT
MAD
THOUGHTS & INSIGHTS
QUALITY AND INTENSITY
FOCUS AND BREATHING
1 — 2 — 3 — 4 — 5 — 6 — 7 — 8 — 9 — 10
VISIONS AND EMOTIONS
REFLECTIONS
I am grateful for ...
I will accomplish ...
I need to work on ...

Notes

WHAT I LIKED

WHAT I DID NOT LIKE

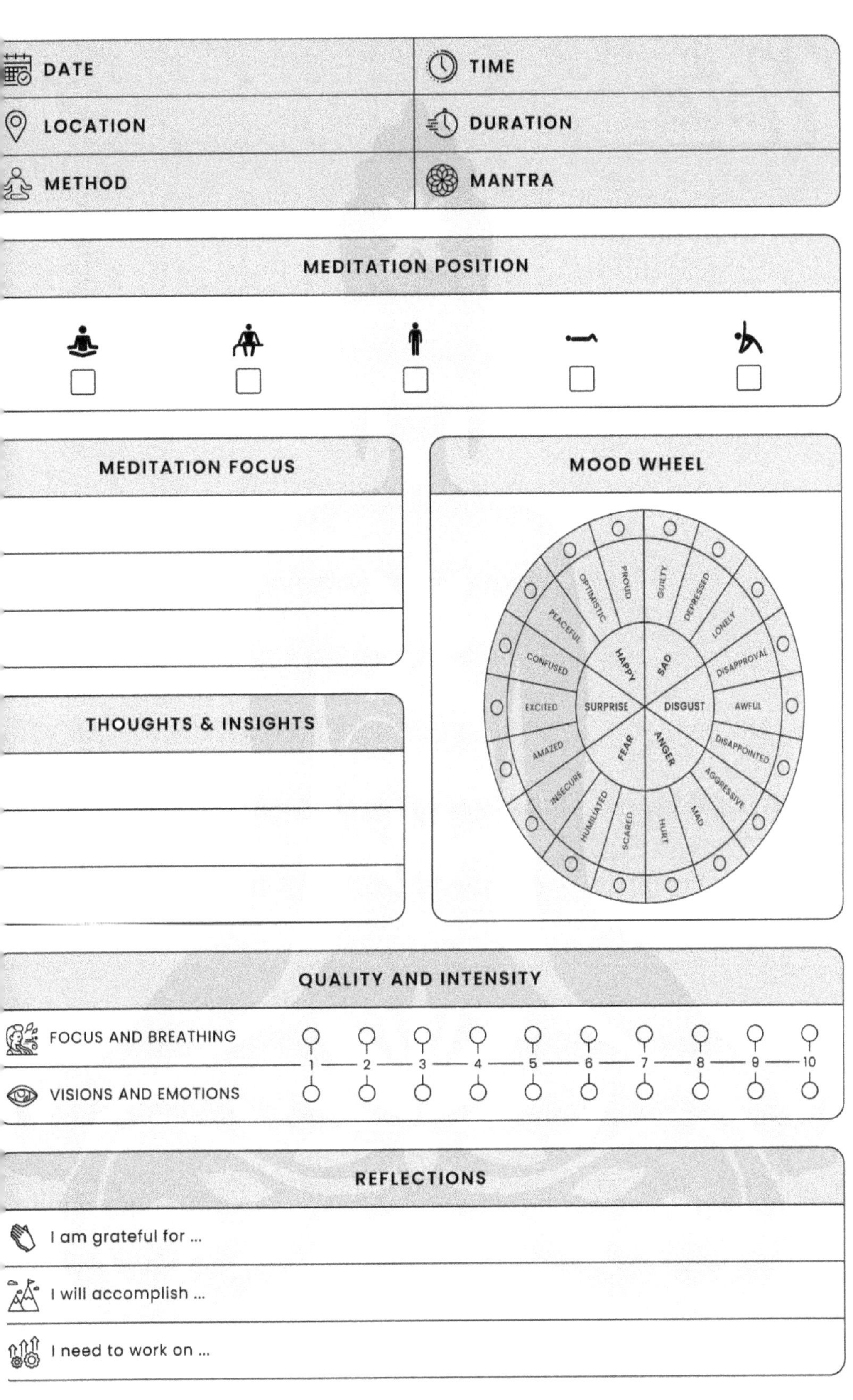

DATE
TIME
LOCATION
DURATION
METHOD
MANTRA
MEDITATION POSITION
MEDITATION FOCUS
MOOD WHEEL
OPTIMISTIC
PROUD
GUILTY
DEPRESSED
PEACEFUL
LONELY
CONFUSED
DISAPPROVAL
HAPPY
SAD
EXCITED
SURPRISE
DISGUST
AWFUL
AMAZED
DISAPPOINTED
FEAR
ANGER
INSECURE
AGGRESSIVE
HUMILIATED
SCARED
HURT
MAD
THOUGHTS & INSIGHTS
QUALITY AND INTENSITY
FOCUS AND BREATHING
1 2 3 4 5 6 7 8 9 10
VISIONS AND EMOTIONS
REFLECTIONS
I am grateful for ...
I will accomplish ...
I need to work on ...

Notes

WHAT I LIKED

WHAT I DID NOT LIKE

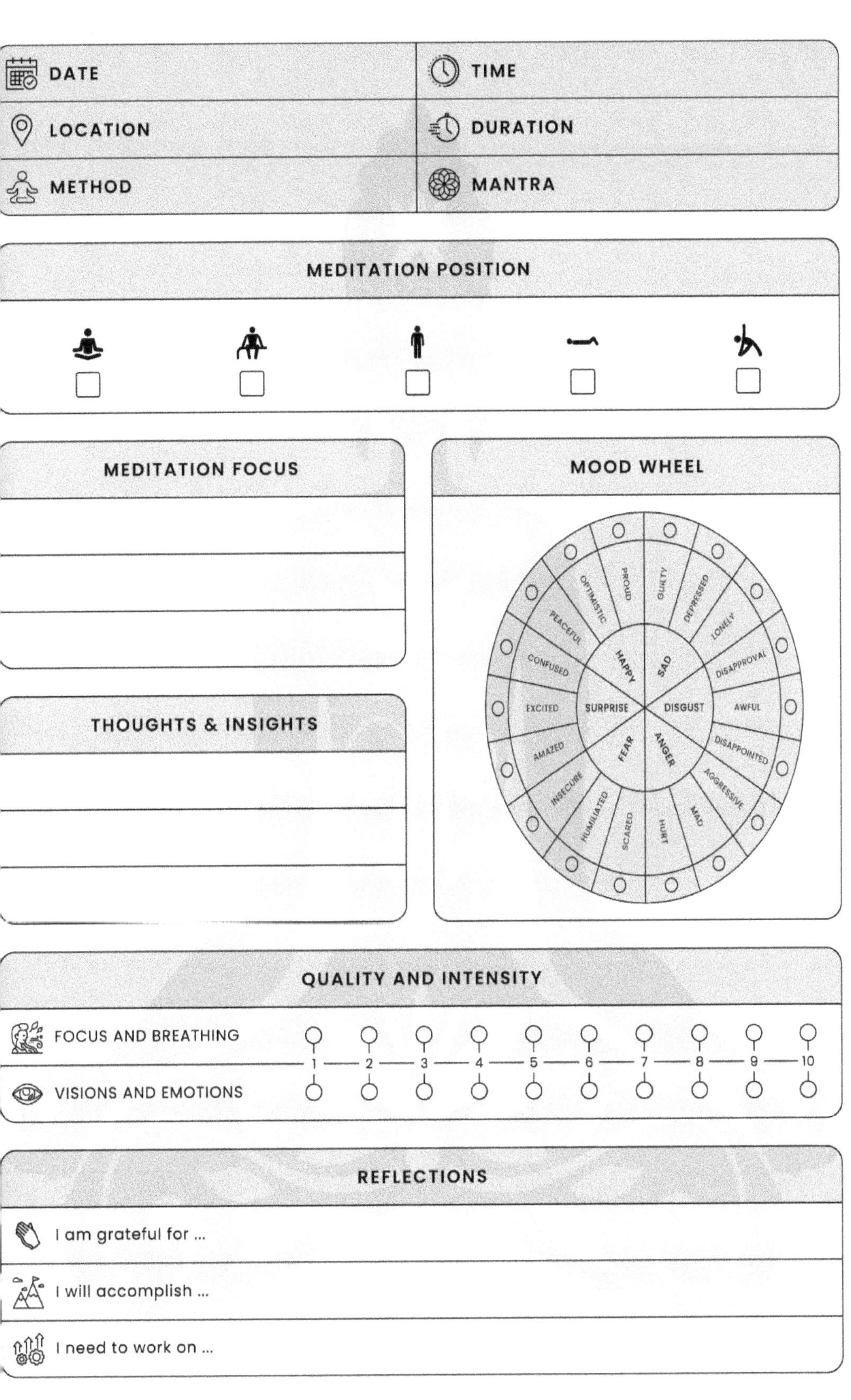

DATE
TIME
LOCATION
DURATION
METHOD
MANTRA

MEDITATION POSITION

MEDITATION FOCUS

MOOD WHEEL

OPTIMISTIC
PROUD
GUILTY
DEPRESSED
PEACEFUL
LONELY
CONFUSED
DISAPPROVAL
HAPPY
SAD
EXCITED
SURPRISE
DISGUST
AWFUL
AMAZED
FEAR
ANGER
DISAPPOINTED
INSECURE
AGGRESSIVE
HUMILIATED
SCARED
HURT
MAD

THOUGHTS & INSIGHTS

QUALITY AND INTENSITY

FOCUS AND BREATHING
1 — 2 — 3 — 4 — 5 — 6 — 7 — 8 — 9 — 10
VISIONS AND EMOTIONS

REFLECTIONS

I am grateful for ...

I will accomplish ...

I need to work on ...

Notes

WHAT I LIKED

____

____

____

____

WHAT I DID NOT LIKE

____

____

____

____

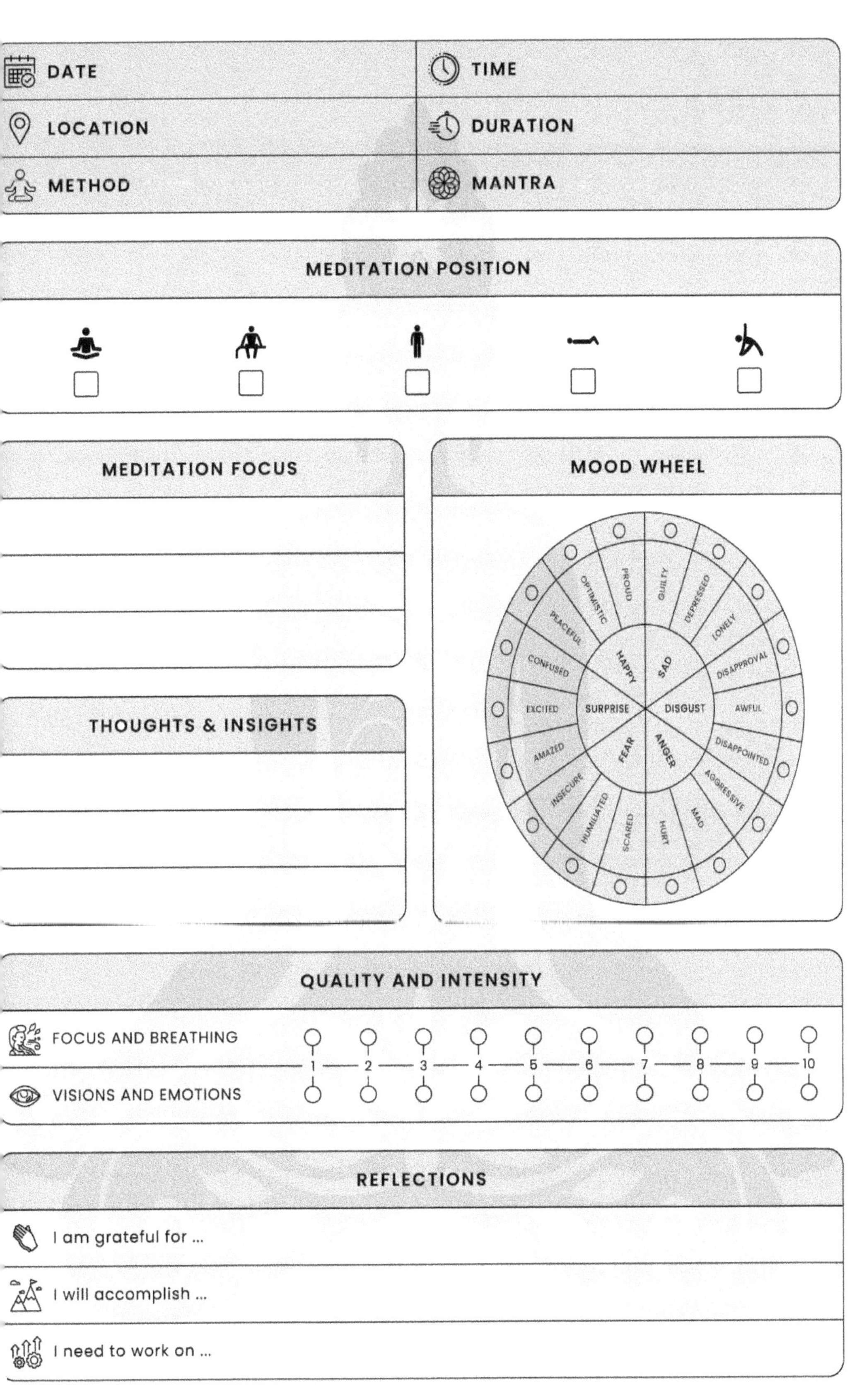

DATE
TIME
LOCATION
DURATION
METHOD
MANTRA

MEDITATION POSITION

MEDITATION FOCUS

MOOD WHEEL

OPTIMISTIC
PROUD
GUILTY
DEPRESSED
PEACEFUL
LONELY
CONFUSED
HAPPY
SAD
DISAPPROVAL
EXCITED
SURPRISE
DISGUST
AWFUL
AMAZED
FEAR
ANGER
DISAPPOINTED
INSECURE
AGGRESSIVE
HUMILIATED
SCARED
HURT
MAD

THOUGHTS & INSIGHTS

QUALITY AND INTENSITY

FOCUS AND BREATHING
1 — 2 — 3 — 4 — 5 — 6 — 7 — 8 — 9 — 10
VISIONS AND EMOTIONS

REFLECTIONS

I am grateful for ...

I will accomplish ...

I need to work on ...

Notes

WHAT I LIKED

WHAT I DID NOT LIKE

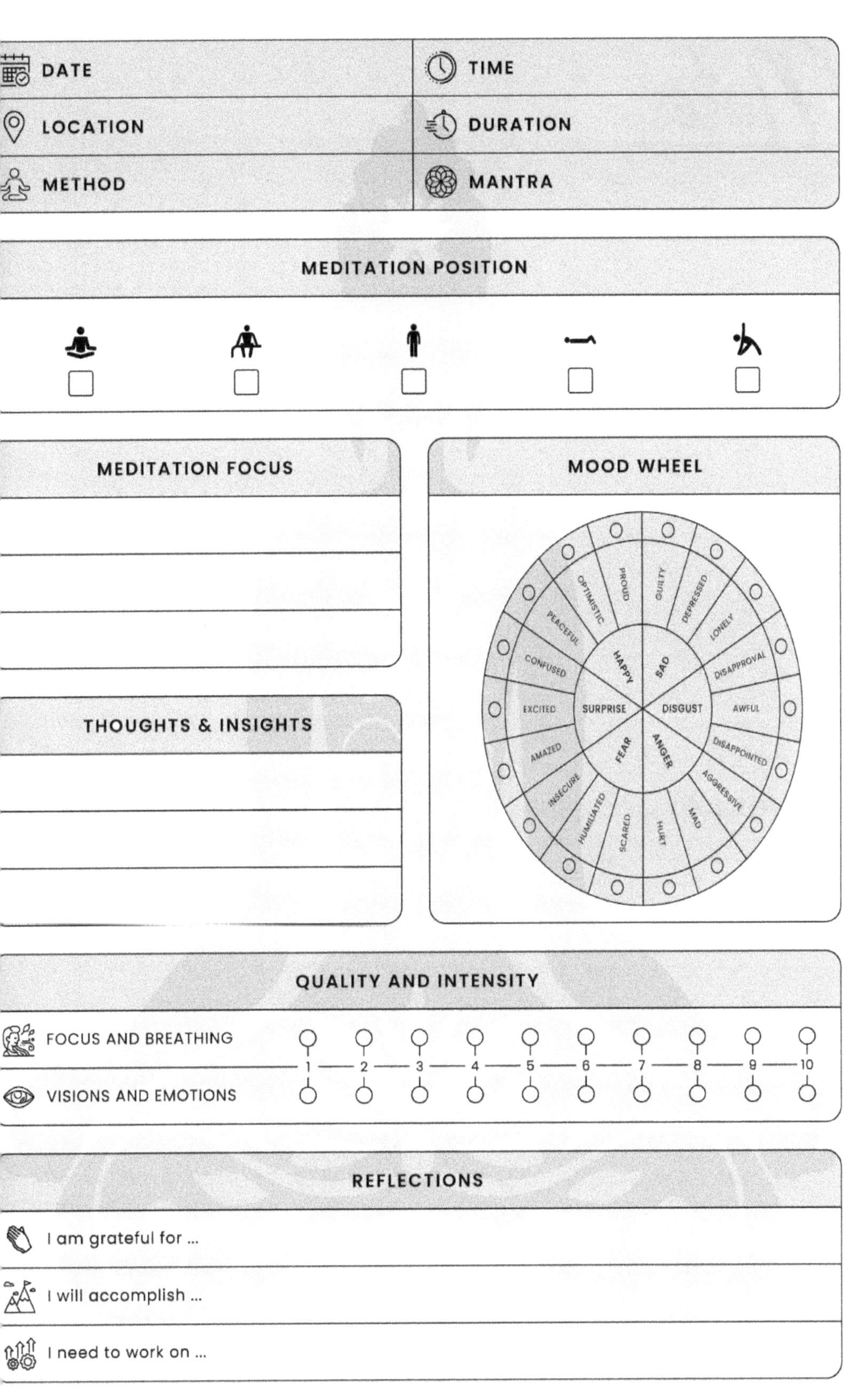

DATE
TIME
LOCATION
DURATION
METHOD
MANTRA

MEDITATION POSITION

MEDITATION FOCUS

MOOD WHEEL

OPTIMISTIC
PROUD
GUILTY
DEPRESSED
PEACEFUL
LONELY
CONFUSED
DISAPPROVAL
HAPPY
SAD
EXCITED
SURPRISE
DISGUST
AWFUL
AMAZED
FEAR
ANGER
DISAPPOINTED
INSECURE
AGGRESSIVE
HUMILIATED
SCARED
HURT
MAD

THOUGHTS & INSIGHTS

QUALITY AND INTENSITY

FOCUS AND BREATHING
1 — 2 — 3 — 4 — 5 — 6 — 7 — 8 — 9 — 10
VISIONS AND EMOTIONS

REFLECTIONS

I am grateful for ...

I will accomplish ...

I need to work on ...

Notes

WHAT I LIKED

WHAT I DID NOT LIKE

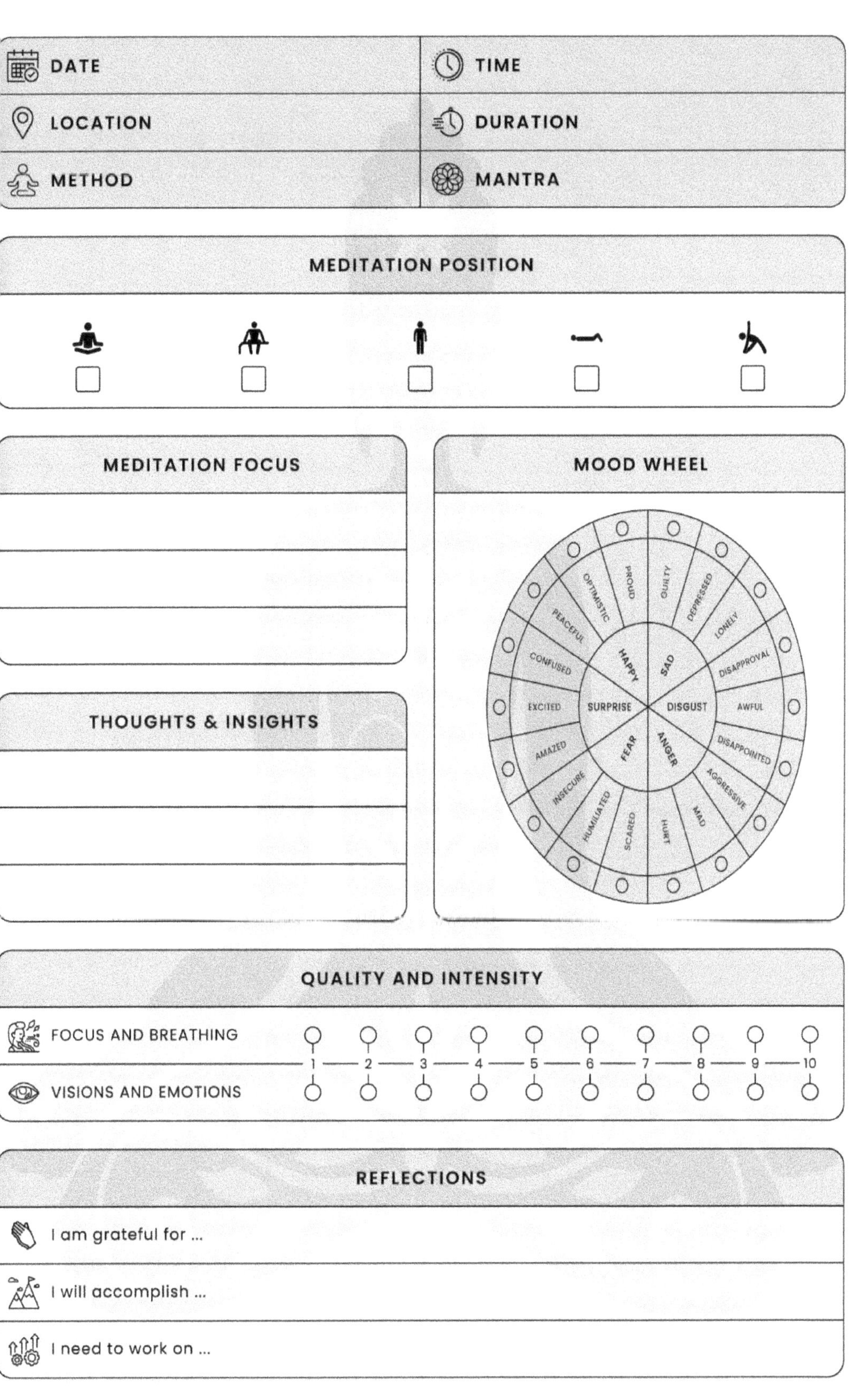

📅 DATE	🕐 TIME
📍 LOCATION	⏱ DURATION
🧘 METHOD	✿ MANTRA

MEDITATION POSITION

☐ ☐ ☐ ☐ ☐

MEDITATION FOCUS

THOUGHTS & INSIGHTS

MOOD WHEEL

QUALITY AND INTENSITY

FOCUS AND BREATHING

1 — 2 — 3 — 4 — 5 — 6 — 7 — 8 — 9 — 10

VISIONS AND EMOTIONS

REFLECTIONS

I am grateful for ...

I will accomplish ...

I need to work on ...

Notes

WHAT I LIKED

WHAT I DID NOT LIKE

📅 DATE	🕐 TIME
📍 LOCATION	⏱️ DURATION
🧘 METHOD	✿ MANTRA

MEDITATION POSITION

☐   ☐   ☐   ☐   ☐

MEDITATION FOCUS

MOOD WHEEL

THOUGHTS & INSIGHTS

QUALITY AND INTENSITY

FOCUS AND BREATHING

1 — 2 — 3 — 4 — 5 — 6 — 7 — 8 — 9 — 10

VISIONS AND EMOTIONS

REFLECTIONS

✋ I am grateful for ...

⛰️ I will accomplish ...

⚙️ I need to work on ...

Notes

WHAT I LIKED

WHAT I DID NOT LIKE

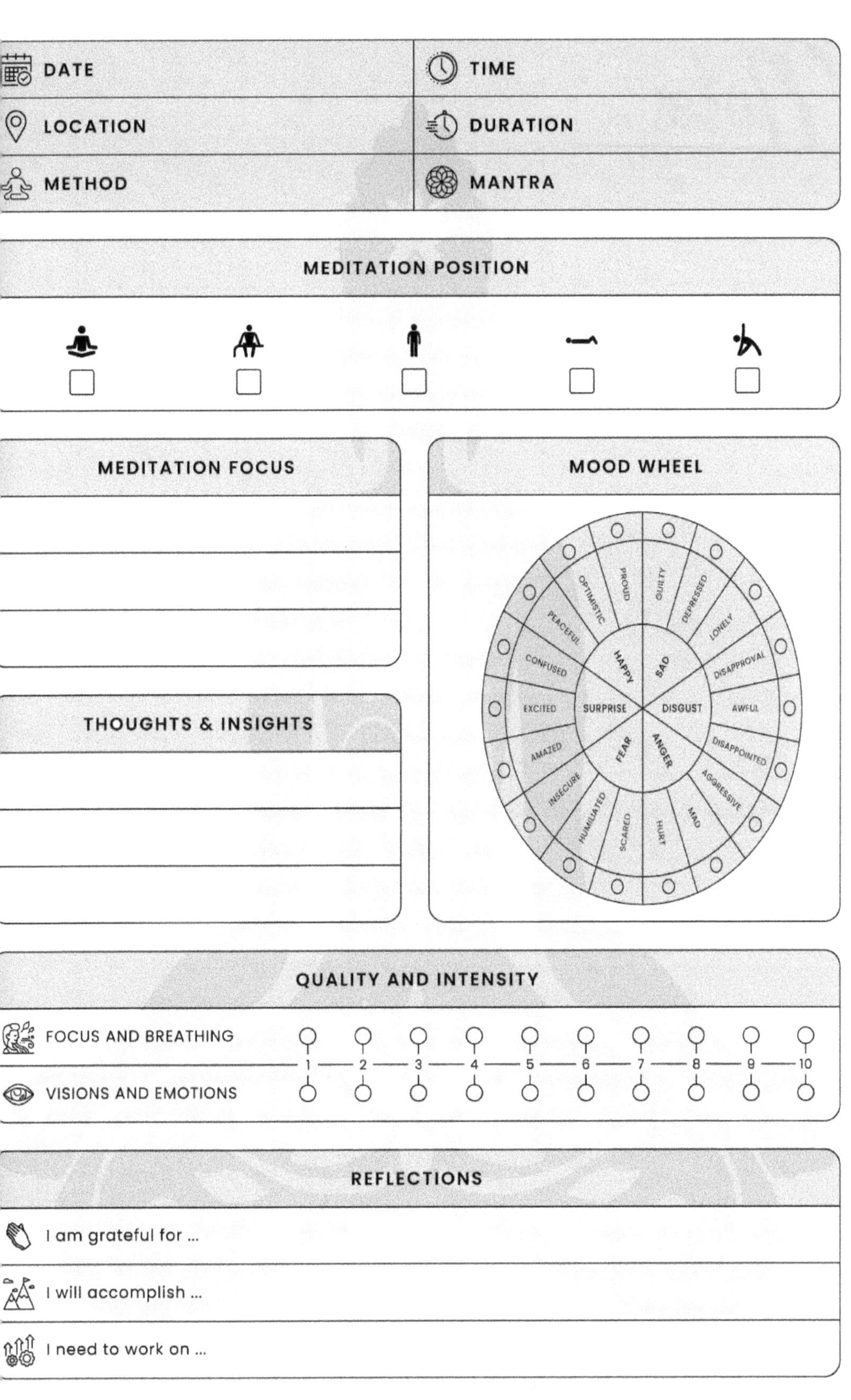

DATE
TIME
LOCATION
DURATION
METHOD
MANTRA
MEDITATION POSITION
MEDITATION FOCUS
MOOD WHEEL
HAPPY
SAD
SURPRISE
DISGUST
FEAR
ANGER
OPTIMISTIC
PROUD
GUILTY
DEPRESSED
PEACEFUL
LONELY
CONFUSED
DISAPPROVAL
EXCITED
AWFUL
AMAZED
DISAPPOINTED
INSECURE
AGGRESSIVE
HUMILIATED
SCARED
HURT
MAD
THOUGHTS & INSIGHTS
QUALITY AND INTENSITY
FOCUS AND BREATHING
1 2 3 4 5 6 7 8 9 10
VISIONS AND EMOTIONS
REFLECTIONS
I am grateful for ...
I will accomplish ...
I need to work on ...

Notes

WHAT I LIKED

WHAT I DID NOT LIKE

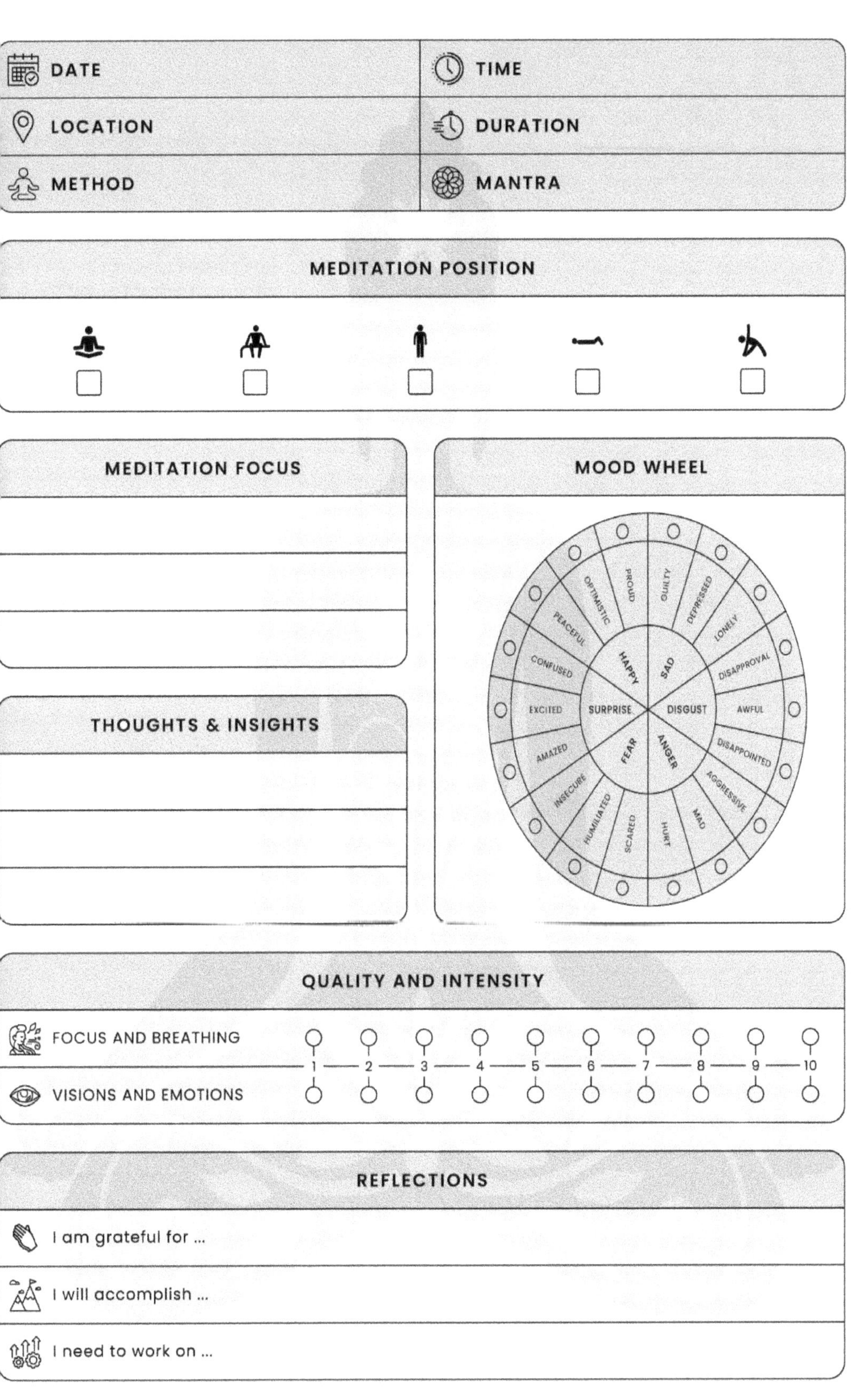

DATE	TIME
LOCATION	DURATION
METHOD	MANTRA

MEDITATION POSITION

☐ ☐ ☐ ☐ ☐

MEDITATION FOCUS

THOUGHTS & INSIGHTS

MOOD WHEEL

QUALITY AND INTENSITY

FOCUS AND BREATHING

1 — 2 — 3 — 4 — 5 — 6 — 7 — 8 — 9 — 10

VISIONS AND EMOTIONS

REFLECTIONS

I am grateful for ...

I will accomplish ...

I need to work on ...

Notes

WHAT I LIKED

WHAT I DID NOT LIKE

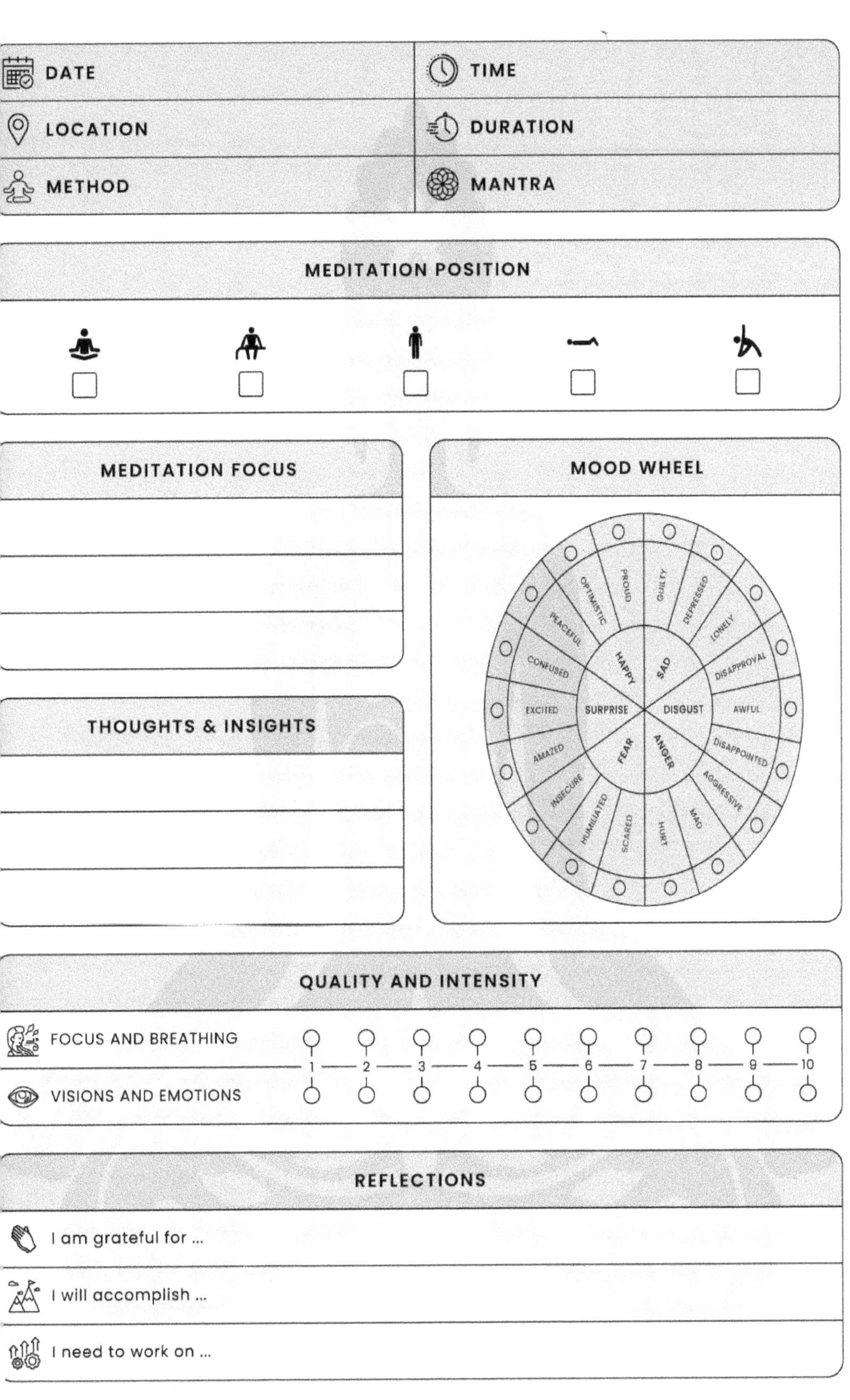

DATE
TIME
LOCATION
DURATION
METHOD
MANTRA

MEDITATION POSITION

MEDITATION FOCUS

MOOD WHEEL

OPTIMISTIC
PROUD
GUILTY
DEPRESSED
PEACEFUL
LONELY
CONFUSED
DISAPPROVAL
HAPPY
SAD
EXCITED
SURPRISE
DISGUST
AWFUL
AMAZED
FEAR
ANGER
DISAPPOINTED
INSECURE
AGGRESSIVE
HUMILIATED
SCARED
HURT
MAD

THOUGHTS & INSIGHTS

QUALITY AND INTENSITY

FOCUS AND BREATHING
1 — 2 — 3 — 4 — 5 — 6 — 7 — 8 — 9 — 10
VISIONS AND EMOTIONS

REFLECTIONS

I am grateful for ...

I will accomplish ...

I need to work on ...

Notes

WHAT I LIKED

WHAT I DID NOT LIKE

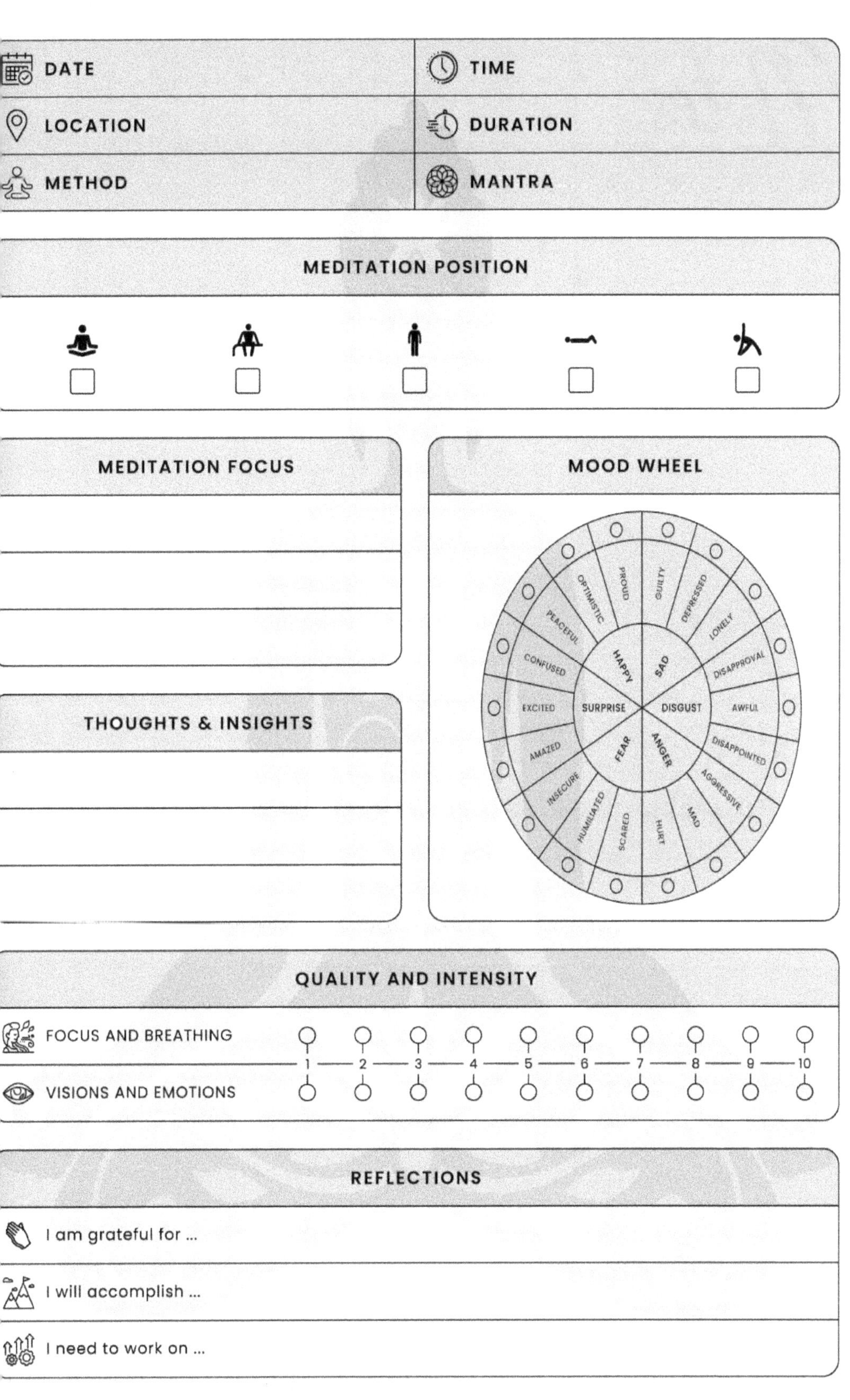

DATE
TIME
LOCATION
DURATION
METHOD
MANTRA

MEDITATION POSITION

MEDITATION FOCUS

MOOD WHEEL

OPTIMISTIC
PROUD
GUILTY
DEPRESSED
PEACEFUL
LONELY
CONFUSED
HAPPY
SAD
DISAPPROVAL
EXCITED
SURPRISE
DISGUST
AWFUL
AMAZED
FEAR
ANGER
DISAPPOINTED
INSECURE
AGGRESSIVE
HUMILIATED
SCARED
HURT
MAD

THOUGHTS & INSIGHTS

QUALITY AND INTENSITY

FOCUS AND BREATHING
1 — 2 — 3 — 4 — 5 — 6 — 7 — 8 — 9 — 10
VISIONS AND EMOTIONS

REFLECTIONS

I am grateful for ...

I will accomplish ...

I need to work on ...

Notes

WHAT I LIKED

WHAT I DID NOT LIKE

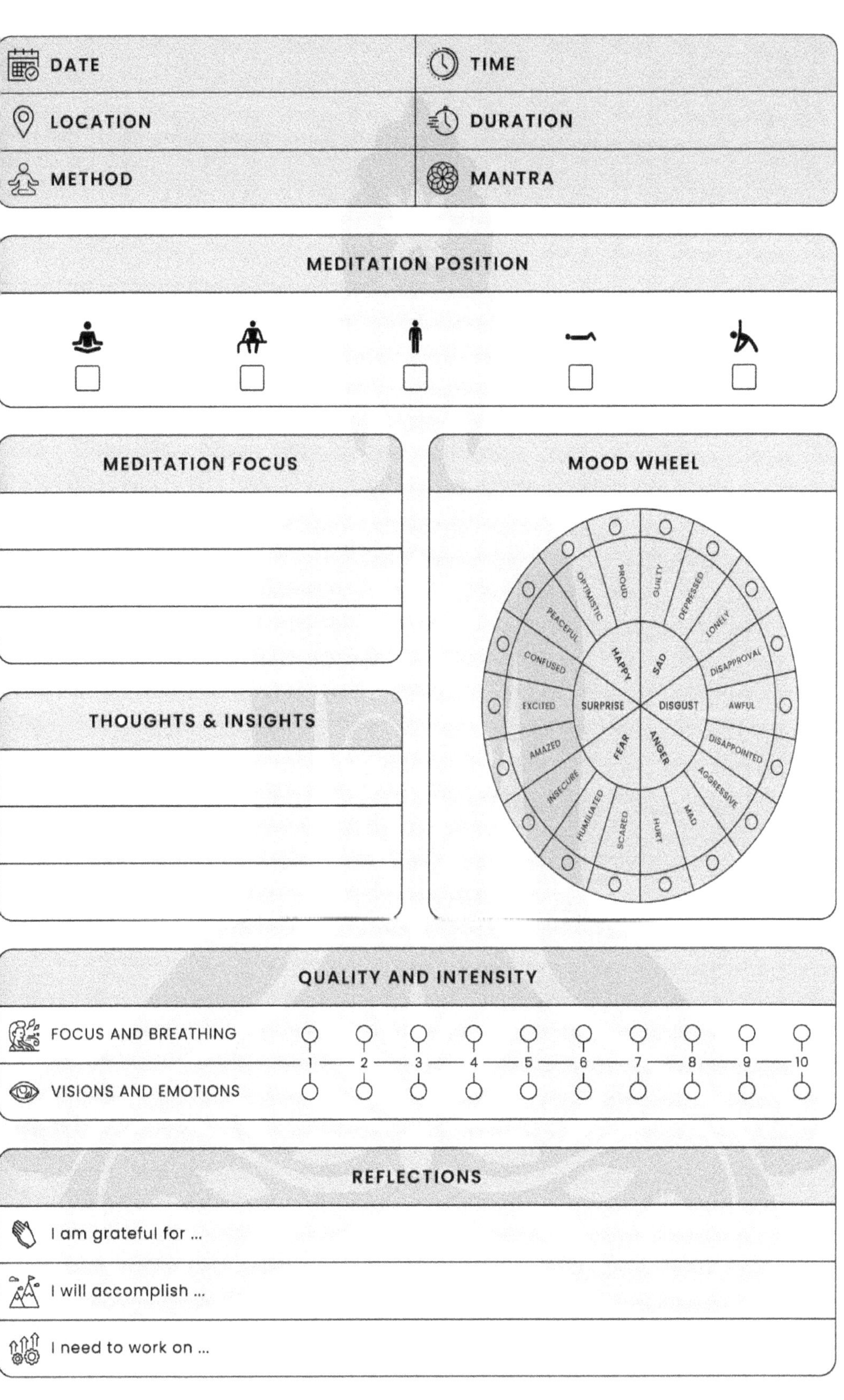
DATE
TIME
LOCATION
DURATION
METHOD
MANTRA

MEDITATION POSITION

MEDITATION FOCUS

MOOD WHEEL

OPTIMISTIC
PROUD
GUILTY
DEPRESSED
PEACEFUL
LONELY
CONFUSED
DISAPPROVAL
HAPPY
SAD
EXCITED
SURPRISE
DISGUST
AWFUL
AMAZED
FEAR
ANGER
DISAPPOINTED
INSECURE
AGGRESSIVE
HUMILIATED
SCARED
HURT
MAD

THOUGHTS & INSIGHTS

QUALITY AND INTENSITY

FOCUS AND BREATHING
1 — 2 — 3 — 4 — 5 — 6 — 7 — 8 — 9 — 10
VISIONS AND EMOTIONS

REFLECTIONS

I am grateful for ...

I will accomplish ...

I need to work on ...

Notes

WHAT I LIKED

WHAT I DID NOT LIKE

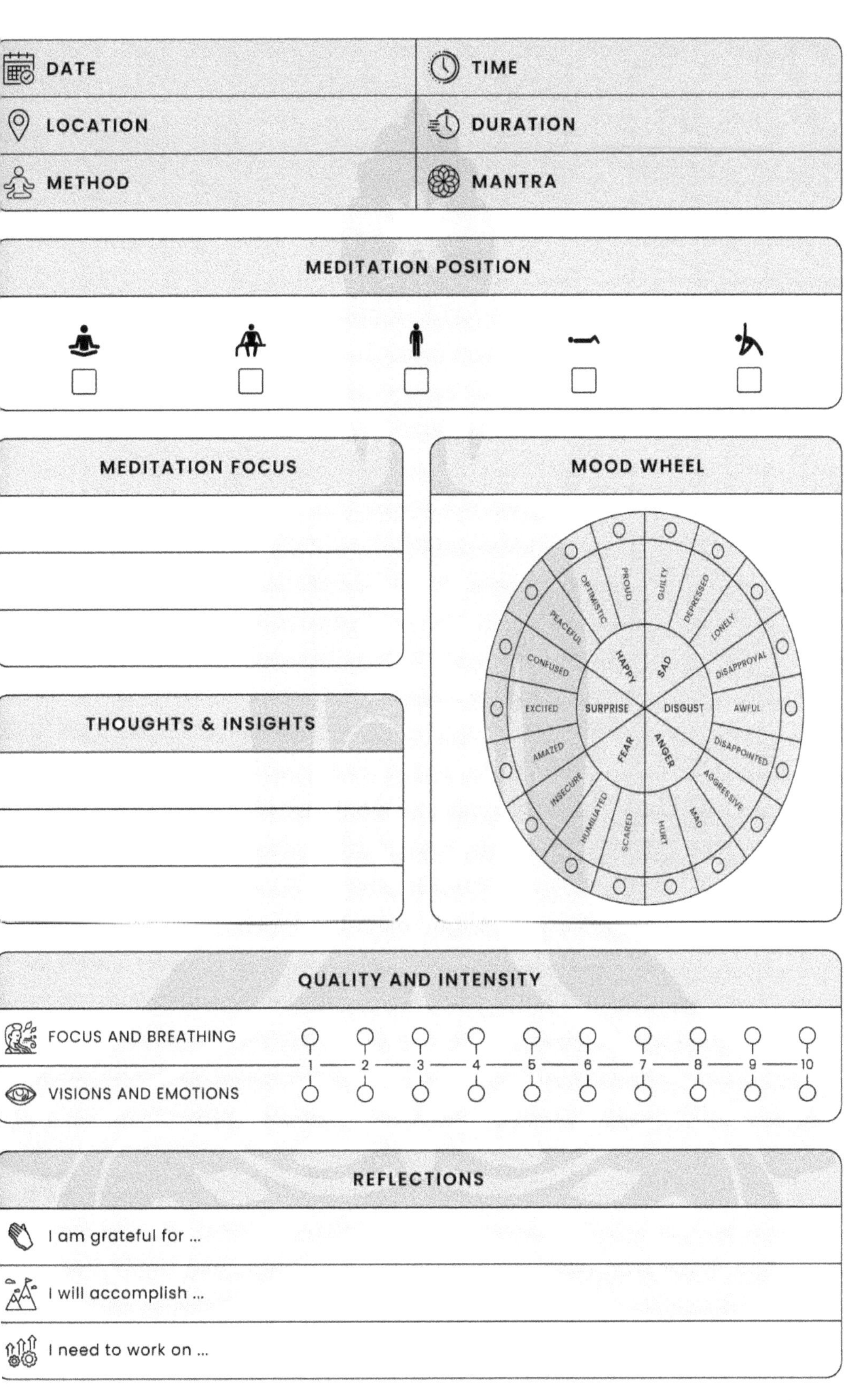

DATE
TIME
LOCATION
DURATION
METHOD
MANTRA
MEDITATION POSITION
MEDITATION FOCUS
MOOD WHEEL
OPTIMISTIC
PROUD
GUILTY
DEPRESSED
PEACEFUL
LONELY
CONFUSED
HAPPY
SAD
DISAPPROVAL
EXCITED
SURPRISE
DISGUST
AWFUL
AMAZED
FEAR
ANGER
DISAPPOINTED
INSECURE
AGGRESSIVE
HUMILIATED
SCARED
HURT
MAD
THOUGHTS & INSIGHTS
QUALITY AND INTENSITY
FOCUS AND BREATHING
1 — 2 — 3 — 4 — 5 — 6 — 7 — 8 — 9 — 10
VISIONS AND EMOTIONS
REFLECTIONS
I am grateful for ...
I will accomplish ...
I need to work on ...

Notes

WHAT I LIKED

____

____

____

____

WHAT I DID NOT LIKE

____

____

____

____

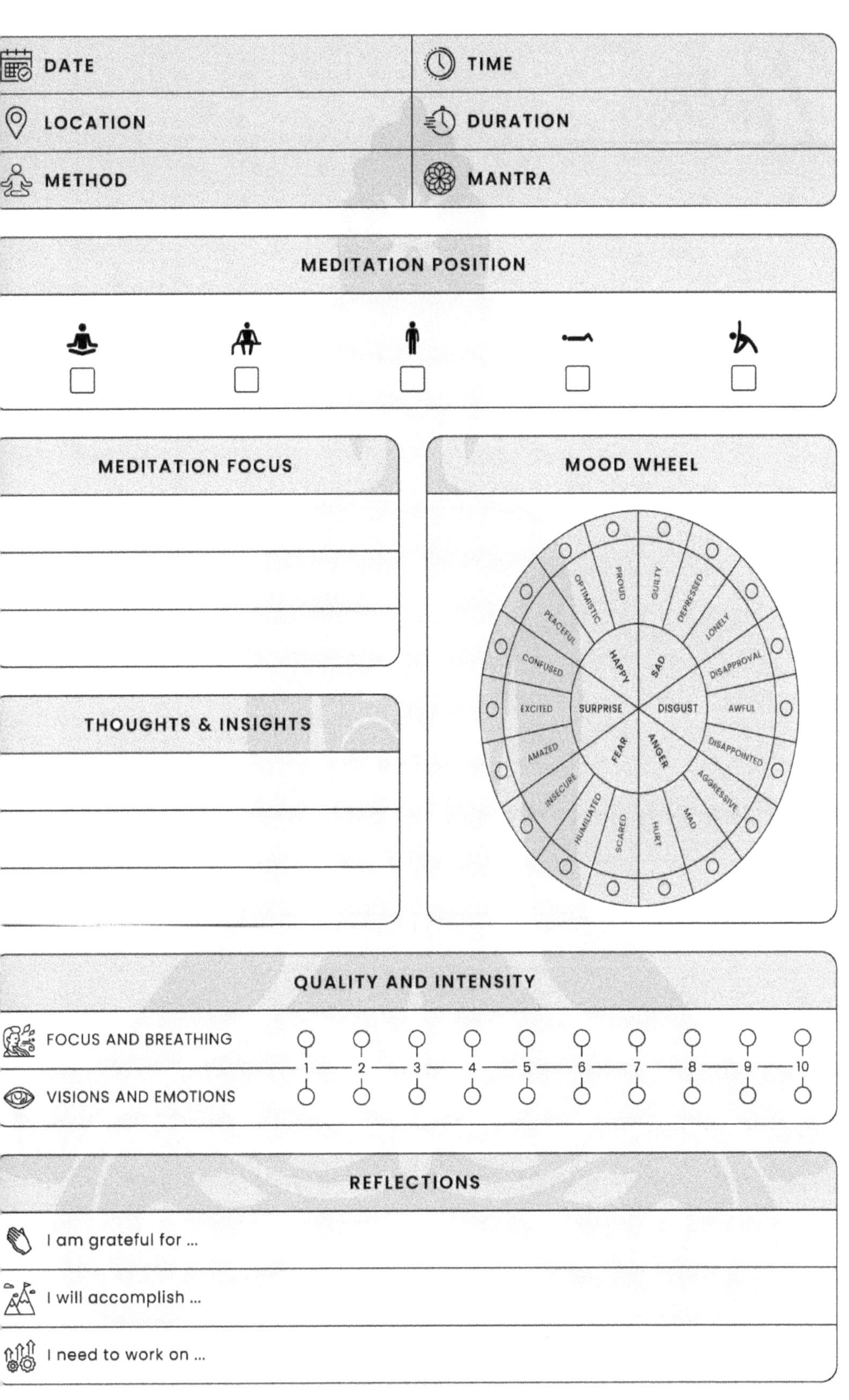

DATE	TIME
LOCATION	DURATION
METHOD	MANTRA

MEDITATION POSITION

☐ ☐ ☐ ☐ ☐

MEDITATION FOCUS

MOOD WHEEL

THOUGHTS & INSIGHTS

QUALITY AND INTENSITY

FOCUS AND BREATHING

1 — 2 — 3 — 4 — 5 — 6 — 7 — 8 — 9 — 10

VISIONS AND EMOTIONS

REFLECTIONS

I am grateful for ...

I will accomplish ...

I need to work on ...

Notes

WHAT I LIKED

WHAT I DID NOT LIKE

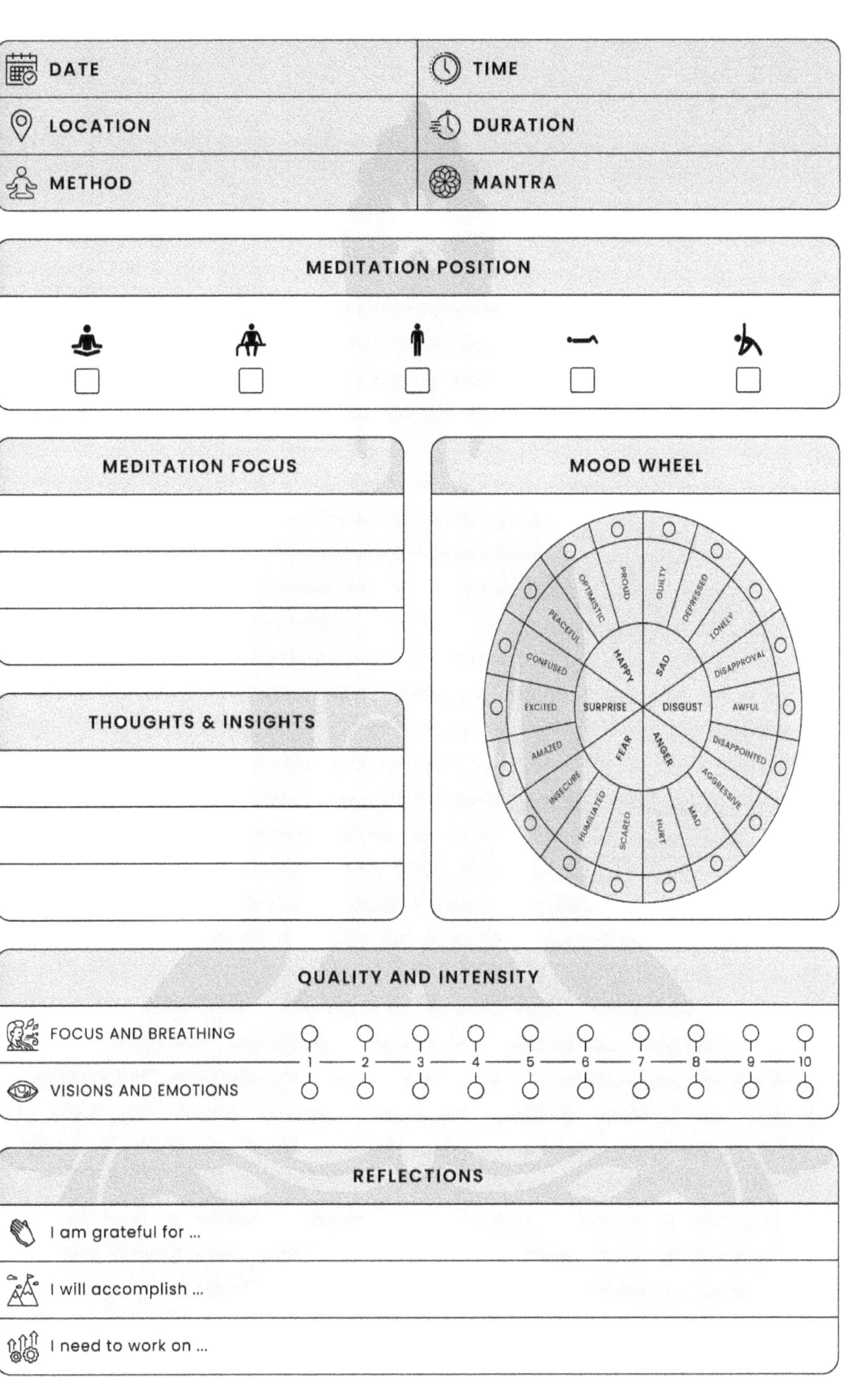

DATE
TIME
LOCATION
DURATION
METHOD
MANTRA
MEDITATION POSITION
MEDITATION FOCUS
MOOD WHEEL
OPTIMISTIC
PROUD
GUILTY
DEPRESSED
PEACEFUL
LONELY
CONFUSED
HAPPY
SAD
DISAPPROVAL
EXCITED
SURPRISE
DISGUST
AWFUL
AMAZED
FEAR
ANGER
DISAPPOINTED
INSECURE
AGGRESSIVE
HUMILIATED
MAD
SCARED
HURT
THOUGHTS & INSIGHTS
QUALITY AND INTENSITY
FOCUS AND BREATHING
1 — 2 — 3 — 4 — 5 — 6 — 7 — 8 — 9 — 10
VISIONS AND EMOTIONS
REFLECTIONS
I am grateful for ...
I will accomplish ...
I need to work on ...

Notes

WHAT I LIKED

WHAT I DID NOT LIKE

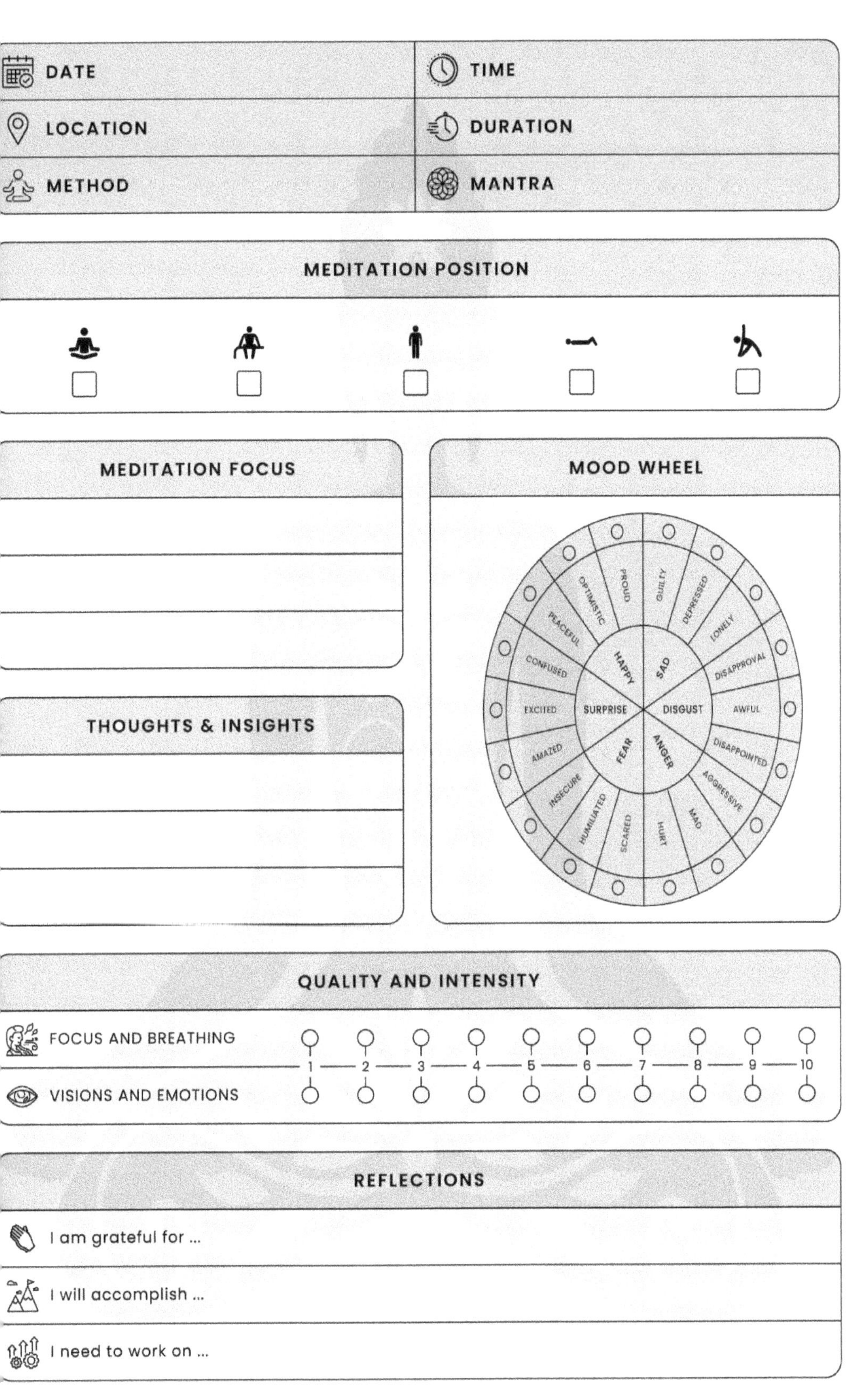

DATE
TIME
LOCATION
DURATION
METHOD
MANTRA

MEDITATION POSITION

MEDITATION FOCUS

MOOD WHEEL

OPTIMISTIC
PROUD
GUILTY
DEPRESSED
PEACEFUL
LONELY
CONFUSED
DISAPPROVAL
HAPPY
SAD
EXCITED
SURPRISE
DISGUST
AWFUL
AMAZED
DISAPPOINTED
FEAR
ANGER
INSECURE
AGGRESSIVE
HUMILIATED
SCARED
HURT
MAD

THOUGHTS & INSIGHTS

QUALITY AND INTENSITY

FOCUS AND BREATHING
1 2 3 4 5 6 7 8 9 10
VISIONS AND EMOTIONS

REFLECTIONS

I am grateful for ...

I will accomplish ...

I need to work on ...

Notes

WHAT I LIKED

WHAT I DID NOT LIKE

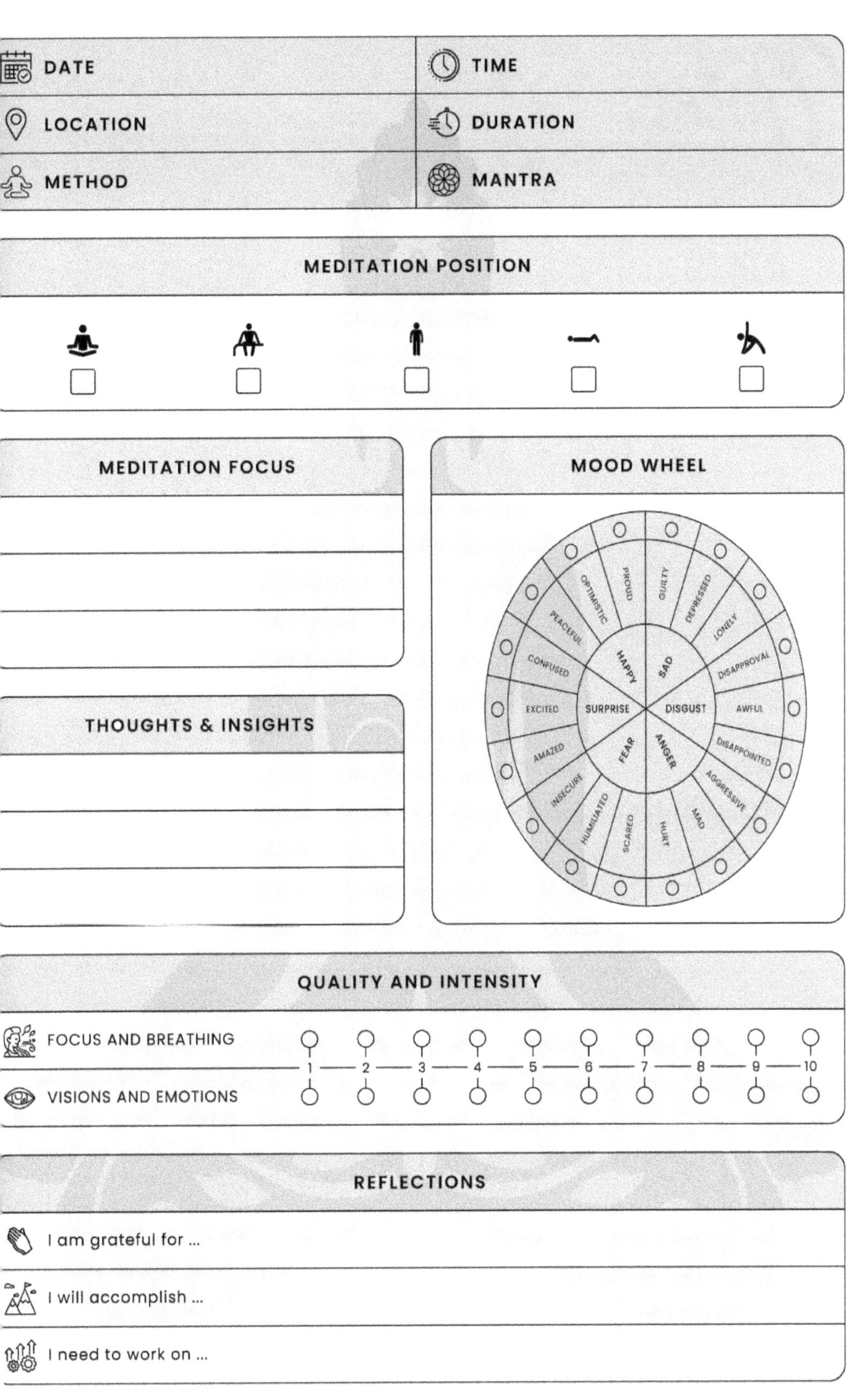

DATE
TIME
LOCATION
DURATION
METHOD
MANTRA
MEDITATION POSITION
MEDITATION FOCUS
MOOD WHEEL
OPTIMISTIC
PROUD
GUILTY
DEPRESSED
PEACEFUL
LONELY
CONFUSED
HAPPY
SAD
DISAPPROVAL
EXCITED
SURPRISE
DISGUST
AWFUL
AMAZED
FEAR
ANGER
DISAPPOINTED
INSECURE
AGGRESSIVE
HUMILIATED
SCARED
HURT
MAD
THOUGHTS & INSIGHTS
QUALITY AND INTENSITY
FOCUS AND BREATHING
1 — 2 — 3 — 4 — 5 — 6 — 7 — 8 — 9 — 10
VISIONS AND EMOTIONS
REFLECTIONS
I am grateful for ...
I will accomplish ...
I need to work on ...

Notes

WHAT I LIKED

WHAT I DID NOT LIKE

MEDITATION POSITION

MEDITATION FOCUS

THOUGHTS & INSIGHTS

MOOD WHEEL

QUALITY AND INTENSITY

FOCUS AND BREATHING

1 — 2 — 3 — 4 — 5 — 6 — 7 — 8 — 9 — 10

VISIONS AND EMOTIONS

REFLECTIONS

I am grateful for ...

I will accomplish ...

I need to work on ...

Notes

WHAT I LIKED

WHAT I DID NOT LIKE

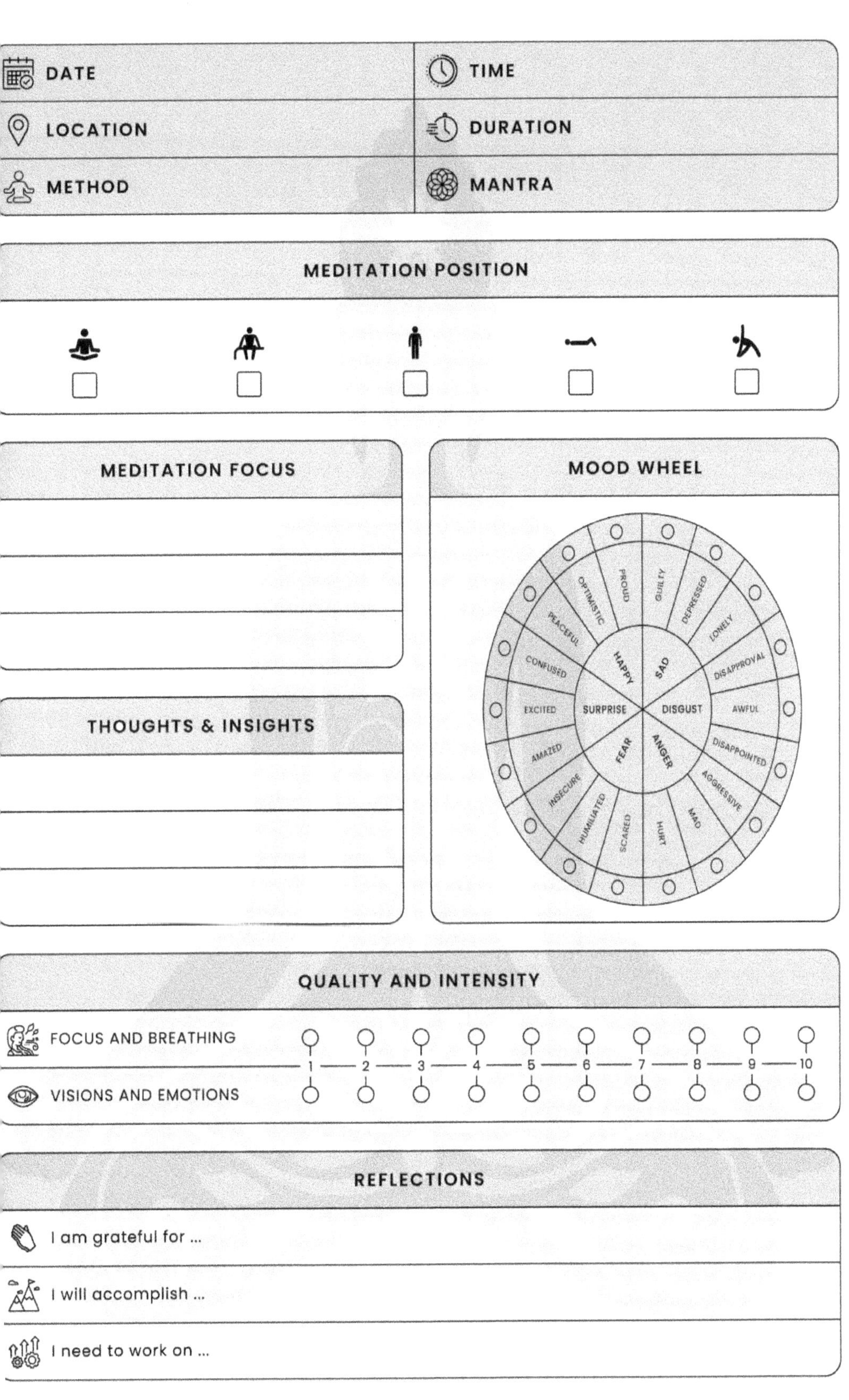

DATE
TIME
LOCATION
DURATION
METHOD
MANTRA

MEDITATION POSITION

MEDITATION FOCUS

MOOD WHEEL

OPTIMISTIC
PROUD
GUILTY
DEPRESSED
PEACEFUL
LONELY
CONFUSED
HAPPY
SAD
DISAPPROVAL
EXCITED
SURPRISE
DISGUST
AWFUL
AMAZED
FEAR
ANGER
DISAPPOINTED
INSECURE
AGGRESSIVE
HUMILIATED
SCARED
HURT
MAD

THOUGHTS & INSIGHTS

QUALITY AND INTENSITY

FOCUS AND BREATHING
1 2 3 4 5 6 7 8 9 10
VISIONS AND EMOTIONS

REFLECTIONS

I am grateful for ...

I will accomplish ...

I need to work on ...

Notes

WHAT I LIKED

WHAT I DID NOT LIKE

<table>
<tr><td>📅 DATE</td><td>🕐 TIME</td></tr>
<tr><td>📍 LOCATION</td><td>⏱ DURATION</td></tr>
<tr><td>🧘 METHOD</td><td>✿ MANTRA</td></tr>
</table>

MEDITATION POSITION

☐ ☐ ☐ ☐ ☐

MEDITATION FOCUS

THOUGHTS & INSIGHTS

MOOD WHEEL

QUALITY AND INTENSITY

FOCUS AND BREATHING

1 — 2 — 3 — 4 — 5 — 6 — 7 — 8 — 9 — 10

VISIONS AND EMOTIONS

REFLECTIONS

🙏 I am grateful for ...

⛰ I will accomplish ...

⚙ I need to work on ...

Notes

WHAT I LIKED

WHAT I DID NOT LIKE

MEDITATION POSITION

DATE	TIME
LOCATION	DURATION
METHOD	MANTRA

MEDITATION POSITION

MEDITATION FOCUS

MOOD WHEEL

THOUGHTS & INSIGHTS

QUALITY AND INTENSITY

FOCUS AND BREATHING

1 — 2 — 3 — 4 — 5 — 6 — 7 — 8 — 9 — 10

VISIONS AND EMOTIONS

REFLECTIONS

I am grateful for ...

I will accomplish ...

I need to work on ...

Notes

WHAT I LIKED

WHAT I DID NOT LIKE

<table>
<tr><td>📅 DATE</td><td>🕐 TIME</td></tr>
<tr><td>📍 LOCATION</td><td>⏱ DURATION</td></tr>
<tr><td>🧘 METHOD</td><td>✽ MANTRA</td></tr>
</table>

MEDITATION POSITION

☐ ☐ ☐ ☐ ☐

MEDITATION FOCUS

THOUGHTS & INSIGHTS

MOOD WHEEL

QUALITY AND INTENSITY

FOCUS AND BREATHING

1 — 2 — 3 — 4 — 5 — 6 — 7 — 8 — 9 — 10

VISIONS AND EMOTIONS

REFLECTIONS

I am grateful for ...

I will accomplish ...

I need to work on ...

Notes

WHAT I LIKED

WHAT I DID NOT LIKE